Dr. T. W. Greenwood MA. MB. FRCP.
West Middlesex University Hospital
Twickenham Road
Isleworth
Middlesex TW7 6AF

OXFORD MEDICAL PUBLICATIONS

Acute Cardiac Care

Acute Cardiac Care

Community and Hospital Management of Myocardial Infarction

Kevin Jennings

Consultant Cardiologist
Royal Infirmary
Aberdeen

OXFORD · NEW YORK · TOKYO
OXFORD UNIVERSITY PRESS
1993

Oxford University Press, Walton Street, Oxford OX2 6DP
Oxford   New York   Toronto
Delhi   Bombay   Calcutta   Madras   Karachi
Kuala Lumpur   Singapore   Hong Kong   Tokyo
Nairobi   Dar es Salaam   Cape Town
Melbourne   Auckland   Madrid
and associated companies in
Berlin   Ibadan

Oxford is a trade mark of Oxford University Press

Published in the United States
by Oxford University Press Inc., New York

A catalogue record for this book is available from the British Library

Library of Congress Cataloging in Publication Data
Jennings, Kevin.
Acute cardiac care: community and hospital management of
myocardial infarction/Kevin Jennings. (Oxford medical publications)
Includes bibliographical references and index.
1. Myocardial infarction.   2. Coronary care units.   3. Coronary
heart disease.   I. Title.   II. Series.
[DNLM: 1. Coronary Care Units—therapy.   2. Myocardial Infarction—
therapy.   WG 300 J54a   1993]
RC685.I6J46   1993   616.1'2—dc20   93-15415
ISBN 0-19-263029-6 (hbk)

Typeset by Advance Typesetting Ltd, Oxford
Printed in Great Britain on acid-free paper by
Biddles Ltd, Guildford & Kings Lynn

For Heather

Inopi beneficium bis dat qui dat celeriter.
(He gives the poor man twice as much good who gives quickly.)
Publilius Syrus, 1st century BC.

Foreword

by Desmond Julian *Medical Director,
British Heart Foundation*

The care of patients with acute myocardial infarction has undergone important changes in the last few years. The introduction of thrombolysis in particular has re-emphasized the importance of treating patients at the earliest possible time after the onset of symptoms. This has been further reinforced by the widespread availability of defibrillators both in the ambulance service and in general practice. In addition to this, the later management has also become clearer, as has the role of rehabilitation, risk stratification, and secondary prevention.

These advances impinge on the work of many different sections of the medical profession, as well as upon nurses, other paramedical personnel and, indeed, the public. The crucial role of the general practitioner, the ambulance service and the Accident and Emergency Department cannot be overstressed.

Dr Jennings's clearly written book will go a long way towards providing the information that health professionals in all these fields will find valuable. Readers will find ample practical advice, supplemented by a useful selection of references for further reading.

Preface

Acute myocardial infarction is the commonest cause of death in the developed world and the majority of these deaths occur out of hospital. There is now clear evidence that prompt coronary care can reduce this mortality significantly. This book describes the management of this condition early in the community and subsequently in hospital: it covers diagnosis, the detection and management of complications, and there is a chapter dealing with cardiological procedures such as the insertion of pacing electrodes and balloon-flotation catheters in addition to elective and emergency cardioversion. There are chapters on recovery and re-habilitation, and on cardiac therapy. At the end of the book I have provided a comprehensive selection of references for those requiring more detail than is provided here.

This book is aimed at all those who manage patients presenting with acute chest pain syndromes and will be relevant particularly to doctors working in the community, and to doctors and nurses employed in accident and emergency departments, coronary care units, and those working in acute medical receiving wards which in Great Britain manage the majority of myocardial infarction.

In writing this book, I have received generous assistance from medical and nursing colleagues at Aberdeen Royal Infirmary which I gratefully acknowledge, and I am indebted to Mr Bruce Mireylees and his staff in the Medical Illustration Department of our Medical School.

April 1993   K. J.
Aberdeen

Contents

1

Epidemiology and pathology

EPIDEMIOLOGY

Coronary disease is the commonest cause of death in developed countries, being responsible for about 30 per cent of total mortality (Dwyer and Hetzel 1980). Annually approximately 270 000 patients experience myocardial infarction in the United Kingdom, from which the majority will die; there are about 180 000 deaths from this cause per year, and 60 per cent of these will occur, usually from ventricular fibrillation, within 2 hours, despite the fact that the median time to arrival in coronary care units is 4 hours. Coronary heart disease is responsible for the premature death of one person under the age of 65 years every 16 minutes in the United Kingdom.

Much information on the potential causation of coronary heart disease is now available to us, and we can make a reasonable distinction between those individuals with a high risk and those with a low risk of developing this disease: the highest-risk population have ten times the risk of the lower-risk group. The British Regional Heart Study (Shaper *et al.* 1984), in a study of 7735 men aged 40–59 years and drawn randomly from general practices in 24 British towns, suggested that 25 per cent of middle-aged men had evidence of coronary disease on questionnaire or ECG evidence. They found that the prevalence rose from 17.6 per cent of those aged 40–44 years to 31.2 per cent in the 55–59 year age-group. In those with both questionnaire and ECG evidence there was a greater rise through this age-range, with the prevalence rising fourfold between 40–44 years and 55–59 years. Further evidence from The British Regional Heart Study indicates that there is a combined acute myocardial infarction or sudden coronary death rate of 6.2 per thousand men aged 40–59 years; this comprises a range from 2.1 per thousand for those aged 40–44 years to 9.6 per thousand for those aged 55–59 years (Shaper *et al.* 1985).

Evidence suggests that in England and Wales there may be 354 000 new cases of coronary heart disease in general practice each year. As many as 27 per cent of new events occur in males aged 45–64 years, although they only represent 11 per cent of the total population (RCGP 1986). There has been a small reduction in the coronary heart disease mortality in Great Britain since 1979, and this is mainly in the age-group 35–44 years and in men. This reduction came after that seen in the United States, Australia, and Finland, whilst France and Japan have continued to benefit from a reduction in coronary heart disease despite having a low baseline prevalence. Countries like Sweden, Poland, Yugoslavia, Romania, Hungary, and the former Soviet Union have experienced an increase in the rate of coronary heart disease.

RISK VARIABLES

Diet: an overview of the epidemiological data available suggests that diet is related to the development of coronary heart disease, possibly as a result of effects on atheroma and thrombosis. Coronary heart disease is infrequently found in those communities which have not adopted a Western diet. Where coronary heart disease is increasingly found in communities where it was once rare it is usually discovered in those who have embraced a more Western lifestyle.

Serum cholesterol is the variable which most determines the geographic distribution of coronary heart disease: in the Seven Countries Study (Keys 1980) death rates from ischaemic heart disease were closely correlated with median cholesterol levels, accounting for 64 per cent of the differences in the ischaemic heart disease rates of the cohorts. Many studies have demonstrated that total serum cholesterol is closely related to the development of ischaemic heart disease, and the relationship occurs for both sexes and is independent of other risk variables. This risk increases through the range of measured cholesterol, so that there is no clear cut-off level: the risk is greater the higher the cholesterol level.

Ischaemic heart disease is closely correlated with the low-density lipoprotein (LDL) fraction: high-density lipoprotein (HDL) may be protective. Plasma lipoproteins are complexes of various lipids with specific proteins known as apolipoproteins. Apolipoproteins serve to interact with phospholipids to help solubilize hydrophobic lipids such as cholesterol; they regulate the reactions of these lipids, and they bind to cell surface receptors to determine the sites of uptake and rates of degradation of the lipids.

Blood-pressure: in the Seven Countries Study (Keys 1980) blood-pressure seemed responsible for about 40 per cent of the geographic variability of ischaemic heart disease mortality. Furthermore, both systolic and diastolic pressure appear as predictors of ischaemic heart disease.

Diabetes: all types of cardiovascular disease appear more frequently in those with diabetes. Diabetic women appear to have similar rates of coronary heart disease to diabetic men, thereby apparently losing the protection against atheroma seen in non-diabetic women.

Obesity: both men and women develop cardiovascular disease more frequently if obese than if non-obese. However this association may not be independent of other factors, and it seems likely that it is hypertension (often associated with the obesity) which is the risk variable for ischaemic heart disease.

Rheological factors: in the Northwick Park Prospective Heart Study men who died of cardiovascular disease showed, at recruitment, significantly higher plasma levels of factor VII, fibrinogen, and factor VIII compared with survivors. Associations with the latter two were at least as strong as for cholesterol. Although not significantly so, fibrinolytic activity was higher in the survivors (Meade *et al.* 1980). These results are supportive of possible hypercoagulability as a risk variable for the development of coronary heart disease.

Exercise: several studies have suggested that vigorous exercise at work or at leisure may protect against coronary heart disease. In a study of 18 000 British civil servants, men who engaged in vigorous physical activity had a coronary heart disease incidence over the next 8.5 years which was half that of those who reported no vigorous exercise (Morris *et al.* 1980). Vigorous exercise was defined as physical activity likely to reach peaks of energy expenditure of 7.5 kcal per minute. The benefit was found regardless of age or whether or not other risk variables for ischaemic heart disease were present. Regular physical activity results in bradycardia and improved cardiac efficacy, but is also associated with favourable effects on HDL cholesterol and fibrinolytic activity which may explain this benefit.

Smoking: many studies have demonstrated that smokers have a higher incidence of, and mortality from, coronary heart disease than non-smokers. The risk appears to be dose-dependent, with the risk being three times greater for heavy smokers than amongst non-smokers. Smoking appears to be an independent risk variable, so that even in hypertensives or those with elevated lipids the risk is higher in smokers than non-smokers. A lower risk exists for reformed smokers, with a greater reduction in the risk the greater the number of non-smoking years.

Stress: it has been suggested that certain people are prone to having a coronary because of their behaviour pattern: so-called Type A personalities are described as striving, aggressive, restless, and ambitious, and their lives are much dictated by time-pressures and deadlines. Studies have reported that such people have more than twice the risk of developing coronary heart disease of Type B personalities, who manifest a more relaxed behavioural pattern (Friedman *et al*. 1982). Not all studies have confirmed this association, however. None the less there is some evidence suggesting that stressful life-events may precipitate myocardial infarction and angina.

Socioeconomic status: although coronary heart disease is more prevalent in richer countries, since the 1950s mortality from this cause has been higher in working-class men. It seems likely that this relates to the less favourable dietary and smoking habits in this population. Although the evidence is not definitive, much research work does support the possibility that psychosocial variables have a causal linkage to coronary heart disease.

Other factors: people who drink alcohol to excess have an increased mortality from coronary heart disease. There is however evidence that drinking moderate quantities of alcohol (up to three drinks per day) is protective against coronary disease, non-drinkers having a higher mortality from coronary heart disease than those who drink within these limits (Marmot 1984). HDL cholesterol levels are known to be increased by alcohol, which may be the mechanism for this protection. It is interesting to note the reduced rates of coronary heart disease in Southern European countries, where the consumption of wine is high.

Some studies have suggested that there is an inverse relationship between coronary heart disease mortality and water hardness—the higher the water hardness, the lower the mortality.

Contrary to popular belief, acute myocardial infarction is more likely to occur at rest than during physical activity: precipitating factors include strenuous exertion in 15 per cent of cases, modest activity in 18 per cent, and surgical procedures in 5 per cent. It may develop in as many as 51 per cent of patients whilst they are at rest, and in 10 per cent of patients whilst they are asleep (Phipps 1936).

PATHOLOGY

Plaque formation and thrombosis

Myocardial infarction results when there is prolonged, unrelieved ischaemia, producing cardiac muscle necrosis. In the majority of cases this results from thrombus formation at the site of a fissured, lipid-rich, atheromatous plaque: these plaques grow by the accumulation of lipid and the formation of connective-tissue matrix proteins, such as collagen, by smooth muscle cells. Following endothelial injury, monocyte accumulation and foam-cell formation result. These monocytes are predominantly macrophages, which are able to release both enzymes and oxygen free-radicals, as well as growth factors which may lead to smooth-muscle cell migration and proliferation. Low-density lipoprotein (LDL), modified by oxidation, and immune mechanisms combine with the proliferation of smooth muscle to produce plaque and narrowing of the arterial lumen. Platelet-derived growth factor (PDGF) is recognized to trigger smooth-muscle proliferation, and monocytes and macrophages contribute to this by production of a PDGF-like substance. Rupture of the plaque allows triggering of platelet aggregation and fibrin deposition. Platelet aggregation enhances lipid uptake and encourages smooth-muscle proliferation. In addition, substances such as serotonin secreted by platelets have an unfavourable effect on vascular tone. Initially the thrombus is mural, allowing forward flow; but it may later become occlusive, and this final thrombus, and any which propagates distally, is rich in fibrin and red cells but contains few platelets. Factors which decide whether or not thrombus will develop after plaque fissuring include the lytic and thrombotic potential of the blood and the area of exposed plaque cap. Large tears, by allowing plaque expansion or extrusion of plaque contents, may cause luminal occlusion independently of thrombus formation; and it is these types of coronary occlusion (in about 15 per cent of myocardial infarction) that are not amenable to thrombolytic therapy.

CORONARY SPASM

The arterial lumen may be central, as a result of concentric intimal thickening, or eccentric, where atheroma has involved only a region of the intima. This leaves a rim of normal arterial wall, which allows for dynamic changes in the tone of the media, and hence alteration in the cross-sectional area of the lumen. This coronary spasm, by reducing coronary flow, can give rise to spontaneous cardiac pain, and may be the mechanism of some unstable angina; although the mechanism in most cases is established to be fissuring of atheromatous plaques with overlying mural thrombus: the cardiac ischaemia results from intermittent thrombotic occlusion or distal embolization of plaque contents. It seems that it is the coronary endothelium which regulates vasomotor tone, using hormones such as endothelin (a powerful constrictor) and endothelium-derived relaxing factor (EDRF), a dilator.

METABOLIC CONSEQUENCES OF INFARCTION

Following total occlusion of a coronary artery contractility declines rapidly, the ECG is altered after approximately 30 seconds, and pain is experienced within about a minute.

Contractile failure associated with ischaemia appears to result from acidosis, impaired sensitivity of contractile proteins to calcium, intracellular accumulation of lipid and phosphate, and a fall in the free energy available for contraction.

There is persuasive evidence that free-radical formation is associated with many of the pathophysiological consequences of ischaemia and reperfusion. These free-radicals (intermediates containing one or more unpaired electrons) are highly reactive and toxic. They result in lipid peroxidation, nucleic acid injury, enzyme inhibition, and ultrastructural damage. Myocardial ischaemia appears to prime the myocardium so that during reperfusion there is a sudden production of oxygen free-radicals, resulting in additional damage. This process continues until it is ended by the scavenging of these free-radicals by antitoxidants. These free-radicals may be responsible for the prolonged, reversible depression of contractility which occurs after ischaemia that we call stunning. There has been considerable interest in the concept of myocardial stunning, whereby myocardium in jeopardy may have reversible injury as a result of reperfusion occurring either naturally or after therapeutic intervention.

Following the onset of acute myocardial ischaemia, the configuration of the action potential changes as a result of alteration of the pH and extracellular potassium, and there is the potential for the development of arrhythmias. This loss of potassium from ischaemic myocardium results from acidosis and reduced activity of the sodium pump, is rapid, and is sufficient to be responsible for the electrophysiological effects occurring early after myocardial infarction.

REPERFUSION

When reperfusion occurs early after the onset of ischaemia there is the potential for full recovery: however, after about 30 minutes of total ischaemia complete functional recovery does not result. Reperfusion is associated with hyperaemia initially; but this initial increased blood-flow diminishes because of increased resistance resulting from cellular oedema, arteriolar spasm, and increased capillary pressure. In prolonged ischaemia reperfusion is not possible, and the 'no-reflow' phenomenon results.

Myocardial haemorrhage may result during reperfusion. It is not certain whether reperfusion damage results from developments occurring during the ischaemia or from developments during the reperfusion following the delivery of oxygen. There is developing evidence that interventions such as heat-stress, cardioplegia, or calcium antagonism, known to limit the damaging effects of ischaemia, are effective only when applied before the onset of ischaemia.

INFARCT SIZE

The ultimate size of the myocardial infarction depends largely on three factors: the area of myocardium at risk; the severity and the duration of the ischaemia; and whether there is residual flow (and the possible recruitment of collaterals will be relevant here) or reperfusion has occurred. Areas of jeopardized myocardium are likely to be greater the more proximal the occlusion, and greater with occlusion of the left anterior descending artery than with closure of the circumflex or right coronary artery; as a result the potential for benefit from therapy is also likely to be greater, because of the larger area of myocardium at risk. The major determinant of collateral supply in acute coronary closure appears to be a pre-existing stenosis: the importance of collateral flow can be seen from the finding that 10 per cent of patients with unstable angina have a completely occluded artery, but no definite infarction, as a result of well-developed collateral circulation (de Zwaan *et al.* 1989).

Approximately 4 per cent of patients with myocardial infarction will have normal coronary arteries, however, and here the presumed mechanism for infarction is coronary spasm or embolism. Prognosis after infarction is closely related to the extent of myocardial damage, so that patients with 40 per cent or more myocardial loss are likely to experience cardiogenic shock, which is associated with a gloomy prognosis (Page *et al.* 1971).

INFARCT TIMING

There is a marked increase in the frequency of myocardial infarction in the morning (Muller *et al.* 1985). Suggested mechanisms for this morning increase include a rise in blood-pressure, resulting in an increase in left ventricular force of contractility; an increase in coronary tone; an unfavourable alteration in platelet aggregability; and a fall in fibrinolytic activity.

Interestingly, in the Physician's Health Study (Ridker *et al.* 1990) aspirin markedly blunted this early-morning peak: in the placebo group a typical circadian variation in the onset of myocardial infarction was seen. In those randomized to receive aspirin there was an overall reduction in the incidence of non-fatal infarction of 45 per cent. This supports the likelihood that it is increased platelet activity which is playing a significant role in the early-morning peak in infarction.

STUTTERING ISCHAEMIA

The sudden development of coronary arterial occlusion without collateral support leads to rapid myocardial death in about 40 minutes: little potential exists for therapeutic intervention during this time-window. However, when there is collateral flow providing an (albeit reduced) blood supply, or if the occlusion does not develop suddenly, then myocardial damage will occur over a longer time-span, allowing more opportunity for intervention.

Support for this phenomenon of stuttering ischaemia is provided by the fact that the surface electrocardiogram often shows changing ST segments in the early phase of infarction, suggesting that blood-flow and therefore ischaemia is varying from moment to moment.

STUNNED MYOCARDIUM

Following myocardial ischaemia, myocardial function and metabolism may not recover for many weeks. The myocardium may remain stunned, with reversibly impaired contractility. Newer scanning techniques able to identify viable, metabolizing myocardium in addition to structure (such as PET scanning) may reveal a role for additional intervention, where apparently dead cardiac muscle is identified to be merely stunned and reversibly ischaemic.

PATHOLOGICAL COMPLICATIONS

Following myocardial infarction, stretching and thinning (infarct expansion) of the infarct site may occur. This results in globular dilatation of the ventricle, with unfavourable consequences for both ventricular and mitral-valve function: it may of course result in cardiac rupture. This development, resulting in pericardial tamponade, is responsible for 10–20 per cent of deaths from myocardial infarction. It is associated with transmural infarction, appears not to be related directly to infarct size, and is more common in older women.

Rupture through the interventricular septum results in the development of left-to-right shunting—a ventricular septal defect. This is more likely to occur in patients who have not previously experienced angina and who do not have well-developed collateral flow. As a consequence the size of the infarction is usually large, and this, associated with the unwelcome haemodynamic burden of the shunt, usually connotes a high mortality.

Necrosis of the papillary muscle occurs commonly in myocardial infarction, and possibly in up to 50 per cent of posterior infarction. Papillary muscle infarction may result in mitral regurgitation, and in a small proportion of all infarction a whole papillary muscle ruptures and the mitral leaflet becomes flail-like and is associated with severe valvular regurgitation. Partial rupture may lead to mitral valve leaflet prolapse and less catastrophic mitral regurgitation. The posterior papillary muscle is more likely to rupture than the anterolateral muscle.

As a legacy of a transmural infarction an aneurysm may form: this protrusion of the ventricular wall consists of collagen throughout its thickness. The aneurysm may be the site of thrombus deposition, may be associated with cardiac failure, and may be the location of threatening cardiac arrhythmias.

Right ventricular infarction occurs in 20—45 per cent of posterior infarcts, and is more likely to occur the more proximal is the occlusion of the right coronary artery. This development may have unfavourable haemodynamic consequences, and is discussed further in the section on **complications** (Chapter 6).

2

Reducing the risk

WHO IS AT RISK FROM CORONARY DISEASE?

It is widely accepted that a combination of risk factors allows for a more accurate prediction of who will develop coronary disease than any isolated risk factor. The variables are: age, sex, cigarette-smoking, blood-pressure, resting ECG abnormalities, serum cholesterol, diabetes, exertional chest pain, and parental death from cardiac disease. These factors allow a degree of risk-stratification in an attempt to identify patients at excess risk of premature cardiac disease so that appropriate advice and therapy can be provided. Such risk-assessment is also useful in persuading patients of the need to make adjustments in their lifestyle and in encouraging them to persevere with therapy. The factors thought to be responsible for coronary heart disease are common in the United Kingdom: 36 per cent of men and 32 per cent of women are smokers, although, with the exception of women aged 15–24, the smoking habit is decreasing. There has been a small reduction in the consumption of saturated fat, with an increase in the consumption of polyunsaturated fat associated with the increase in the use of soft margarine. Coronary heart disease is of multifactorial origin, and we should avoid concentrating on any one risk factor in isolation. This is particularly true of cholesterol, where testing should be performed in association with assessment of other risk variables.

RISK-ASSESSMENT

Risk-assessment should include the following:

● Noting if there is a family history of premature coronary heart disease.

● Recording the blood-pressure and advising on the need for weight loss or reduction in salt or alcohol in the diet if this likely to be a factor. Patients should only be considered for blood-pressure lowering therapy where it is significantly and persistently elevated. The British Hypertension Society have provided guidelines for the management of hypertension (Swales *et al.* 1989): men and women under 80 whose diastolic blood-pressure averages 100 mm Hg or more over three to four months should be considered for drug therapy.

● Noting if the patient is a smoker, followed by advice on the risks and the need to surrender this habit.

● Cholesterol measurement should be performed in those under the age of 50 with xanthoma, corneal arcus, or xanthelasma, and also in those with a family history of premature coronary heart disease. It should be performed in those with diabetes or hypertension, and in those who present relatively young with symptoms of coronary disease such as angina and myocardial infarction (but not for three months after infarction, as lipid profiles are unreliable during this interval).

Those with ischaemic heart disease who are at special risk of myocardial infarction or death are patients with unstable angina: see **unstable angina**, Chapter 3.

There is some evidence to suggest that a reduction in the prevalence of coronary heart disease is feasible by a favourable alteration of those risk factors mentioned above which are amenable to manipulation.

In the United Kingdom there is the opportunity to provide screening and lifestyle advice through the primary health-care system: 95 per cent of people are registered with a general practitioner and 90 per cent of people consult their practitioner in a five-year period, and approximately 70 per cent in any one year.

RECOMMENDATIONS

The British Cardiac Society (1987) have recommended the following:

● Every opportunity should be taken to influence the population to eliminate cigarette-smoking, particularly in young people.

● Those with blood cholesterol levels above 6.5 mmol/litre should receive dietary advice, and some patients with levels above 7.8 mmol/l may require drug therapy in addition to dietary advice. So far as dietary advice is concerned, the Society endorses the recommendations of the Committee on Medical Aspects of Food Policy (1984). In essence this is that the consumption of fat in the diet should be reduced so that there is no more than 35 per cent of food energy from total fat and 15 per cent of food energy from saturated fat. The ratio of polyunsaturated fatty acids to saturated fatty acids should be increased to 0.45. There should be an increase in fibre-rich carbohydrates to compensate for the reduced intake of fat. Particular attention should be given to the provision of a healthy diet as identified above to children over the age of five.

● While the lowering of elevated blood-pressure by drug treatment has not been shown persuasively to reduce the incidence of myocardial infarction, the favourable effects on the cerebrovascular circulation are undoubted, and those with diastolic pressures over 100 mm Hg should be considered for therapy, and have their other risk factors addressed.

● Obesity in adults and children should be avoided by appropriate diet and regular exercise.

● Physical activity should be encouraged.

The British Cardiac Society further suggest that cardiologists, consultant physicians, general practitioners, health authorities, and related professionals should assume a more active role than in the past in order that these recommendations might be implemented.

There is persuasive epidemiological evidence, then, linking factors such as smoking, elevated blood-pressure, and hyperlipidaemia to coronary heart disease; they allow assessment of the relative risk within a population, but are weak in their ability to define risk in the individual. Those with a level of cholesterol or blood-pressure towards the upper end of the population distribution certainly have a significantly higher risk compared with those people who have lower levels; but the individual risk is not the same for everyone: the 20 per cent of healthy men aged 40–55 years who have the highest risk because of elevated cholesterol and blood-pressure contain within their midst a majority (actually two-thirds) who will not develop coronary disease over the following 25 years. To implement a high-risk strategy only would be to ignore the fact that most coronary heart disease occurs in the much larger population of those who are at only moderate risk, and who might then have benefit withheld. We should also bear in mind that trials of multiple risk-factor intervention have been largely disappointing, and that trials to lower lipids, while resulting in reduction of coronary heart-disease incidence, have not been shown to reduce total mortality.

Furthermore, blood-pressure reduction studies have not demonstrated a reduction in coronary-disease incidence. While one of the possible explanations is that these studies were started too late in the natural history of the disease process, and too little follow-up time was involved to allow a positive result to be achieved, some lipid-lowering studies have shown an increase in non-cardiovascular mortality and, interestingly, an excess of violent death in treated groups.

THE CHOLESTEROL DEBATE

The association of elevated cholesterol with increasing risk of coronary heart disease is well established, and there is consensus about a reduced risk of cardiac events with reduction in cholesterol levels reported from several studies. The continuing debate relates to the controversy surrounding the increase in non-cardiac deaths that has been revealed in these studies (Smith and Pekkanen 1992). As has been indicated in this chapter, the official recommendations are for an aggressive reduction in cholesterol levels for the primary prevention of coronary heart disease, and indeed the European Atherosclerosis Society recommends a level of cholesterol above which they recommend that lipid-lowering agents should be considered which is well below the mean population cholesterol level.

There is accumulating evidence that atherosclerosis in humans is reversible. The POSCH study (the Programme on the Surgical Control of the Hyperlipidemias) was designed to investigate whether the cholesterol reduction resulting from partial ileal bypass surgery would have a favourable impact on cardiac mortality and morbidity (Buchwald *et al*. 1990). In this study 838 patients were randomized who had survived a first myocardial infarction and who had a total cholesterol of at least 220 mg/dL. At five-year follow-up the surgical group had a total cholesterol level 23.3 per cent lower than that in the control group. While total mortality was not significantly reduced, cardiac death and non-fatal reinfarction combined was significantly lower, by 35 per cent. Overall mortality in the surgical group for patients with an ejection fraction greater than 50 per cent was significantly lower by 36 per cent, and during follow-up twice the number of control patients underwent coronary surgery compared with the surgical group. A comparison of baseline coronary arteriograms compared with those performed at 3, 7, 5, and 10 years consistently showed less disease progression in the surgically managed group. These results provided good evidence for the benefit of lipid-lowering in the reduction of atherosclerotic progression. The advent of powerful lipid-lowering drugs has reduced the need for surgical management of hyper-cholesterolaemia.

In the Familial Atherosclerosis Treatment Study (FATS), 146 men with a family history of coronary heart disease and elevated apolipo-protein B were randomly allocated to one of three lipid-lowering regimes (Brown *et al.* 1990). All patients had evidence of coronary disease, with a baseline arteriogram showing at least one 50 per cent stenosis or three 30 per cent stenoses. The regimes were niacin–colestipol, lovastatin–colestipol, and conventional therapy with pla-cebo. Matched cineangiograms were obtained at baseline and two and a half years later. In the conventional treatment group 46 per cent of the patients had definite lesion progression (and no regression), and regression was the only change in 11 per cent. In contrast, progression as the only change was less frequently seen in the two treatment groups (21 per cent for lovastatin–colestipol and 25 per cent for niacin–colestipol). Regression was more frequent in these treatment groups: 32 per cent in the lovastatin–colestipol group and 39 per cent in the niacin–colestipol-treated patients. Clinical events such as death, myocardial infarction, or revascularization occurred in 10 of 52 patients treated with conventional therapy, and in 3 of 46 patients allocated to lovastatin–colestipol and in 2 of 48 who received niacin–colestipol: the relative risk of an event during lipid-lowering therapy being 0.27, with 95 per cent confidence limits of 0.10–0.77.

The available evidence does support the possibility that significant lowering of lipids can inhibit progression of atherosclerosis in humans, and can even result in regression of disease. There appears to be an increase in non-cardiovascular deaths associated with lipid-lowering therapy; intriguingly, much of this increase is associated with violence and trauma. However when the results of the major trials are pooled (Smith and Pekkanen 1992) death from injury is not significantly increased in the treatment groups of the dietary trials (odds ratio 1.20; $p = 0.4$). But in the treatment groups of the drug trials there is a marked increase in the odds ratio for death from injury (odds ratio 1.75; $p = 0.026$), although the difference between these two odds ratios is not significant, based as they are on a relatively small number of deaths. When all non-cardiac deaths are analysed, mortality from these causes is substantially and significantly raised in the drug trials, but not in the dietary studies.

The results of the first year of follow-up for all-cause mortality in the EXCEL trial are disturbing: in this study, using the powerful lipid-lowering agent lovastatin (a HMG CoA reductase inhibitor), 0.5 per cent of patients receiving drug treatment died, compared with 0.18 per cent of patients taking placebo (Bradford *et al.* 1990).

In general the cholesterol levels in the drug trials were higher than in the dietary studies, and it could be anticipated therefore that there would be more likelihood of benefit in the drug studies: lowering of cholesterol has the highest potential benefit in those with the greatest cholesterol concentrations. These authors recommend that these agents are reserved in general for patients with severe, familial hyper-lipidaemia, where the benefit more clearly outweighs the adverse effects.

In a recent editorial, Oliver (1992) raised doubts concerning the value of lipid-lowering in middle-aged men. The editorial was stimulated by the report of a trial designed to prevent coronary heart disease in middle-aged Finnish men (Strandberg *et al.* 1991). This study found that over the ten-year period after the study ended cardiac deaths and total mortality increased progressively in the intervention group compared with the control patients. The editorial commented that this finding combined with the reports of an increase of non-cardiac deaths related to drug therapy for treatment of hypercholesterolaemia should make us reconsider current policies for the primary prevention of coronary heart disease.

In this Finnish study, 1222 men with more than one risk variable for coronary disease were randomized to intervention and control groups. Those allocated to the intervention group were reviewed regularly, received advice about diet, smoking, and physical activity, and were treated for hypertension or hyperlipidaemia if present. Five years later, intervention ended, at which time the predicted coronary heart-disease risk had been almost halved in the intervention group. None the less, more non-fatal myocardial infarction and cardiac deaths occurred in the intervention group. The study group were followed up for 10 more years: among the men who had been allocated to the intervention group total mortality, cardiac mortality, and violent deaths were increased significantly. No clear and credible explanation has been proposed for these surprising findings, and the increased rate of violent deaths in the intervention group is in keeping with reports of other lipid-lowering trials—a finding Professor Oliver says we should neither ignore nor dismiss merely because we cannot explain it.

He does allow, however, that rigorous intervention directed specific-ally at smoking and reducing elevated cholesterol by diet may be effective: the Oslo study of men with high initial levels of cholesterol (7.5–9.8 mmol/litre) and high average daily fat intake showed benefit at five years. At eight and a half years the rate of fatal cardiac events had been halved. This study involved a strict diet with the poly-unsaturated:saturated fat ratio > 1.0 (Hjermann *et al.* 1981).

The editorial concludes that the available evidence gives little support to the idea that a change in the lifestyles of the middle-aged will have a significant impact on total mortality or cardiac deaths, and that we may be too little and too late by beginning prevention in middle age. We should however energetically treat those at particularly high risk from coronary heart disease—those with familial hyperlipidaemia—and advise against cigarette-smoking in all, as the evidence for this is secure.

Familial hyperlipidaemia

Patients with familial hyperlipidaemia have an especially high risk of coronary heart disease. This autosomal dominant disorder is character-ized by hypercholesterolaemia, tendon xanthomas, and premature coronary disease. Heterozygous familial hyperlipidaemia affects approximately 1:500 in the United Kingdom, and plasma cholesterol shows little response to dietary change. Over half the male hetero-zygotes and 15 per cent of women die aged less than 60 years.

Hypertriglyceridaemia

Studies of the association of elevated triglycerides and coronary heart disease have shown that this is independent of total cholesterol, but that the triglyceride association may not persist when the analysis is controlled for HDL cholesterol. Randomized studies have not been performed looking specifically at reduction of triglycerides: multi-variate analysis in those studies which while being directed at choles-terol also had a lowering effect on triglycerides have shown lower rates of coronary disease associated with decrease in total or LDL cholesterol and increases in HDL cholesterol—but not with changes in triglyceride levels.

The role of reduced triglycerides in reducing the rate of coronary heart disease has not been convincingly established, and therapy for asymptomatic hypertriglyceridaemia cannot be recommended presently. In patients with high triglyceride levels who are symptomatic with eruptive xanthomata or pancreatitis therapy may be appropriate.

WORK ENVIRONMENT

It has been calculated that 16 per cent of the premature cardiovascular mortality in men and 22 per cent in occupationally active women is avoidable through interventions in the work environment (Olsen and Kristensen 1991). Furthermore, if sedentary work is included in occupational risk factors the aetiological fractions reach 51 per cent for men and 55 per cent for women. The major aetiological fractions for cardiovascular risk at work (women in brackets) are: monotonous high-paced work 6 per cent (14 per cent), shift work 7 per cent (7 per cent), and passive smoking 2 per cent (2 per cent). The authors conclude that working conditions play a considerable role in the development of cardiovascular disease: they invite the focusing of preventive measures on working conditions, in addition to the usual individual and lifestyle risk variables.

SCREENING

A particular effort should be made to attempt to find those who are at excess risk of coronary heart disease so that steps may be taken to reduce their risk. To attempt to screen the whole population would be expensive and is not practical; the alternative, which is to identify those who are at the highest risk, is more attractive, even though this will only identify a minority of those at risk. This opportunistic screening when patients present to general practitioner or hospital, usually for treatment for non-cardiological conditions, is a reasonable compromise which should be encouraged. It should involve:

● taking blood for cholesterol analysis from the young who have a family history of premature coronary heart disease and from first-degree relatives of those with hyperlipidaemia; and

● all patients having their blood-pressure measured at least once in a five-year period.

3

Unstable ischaemia

Angina is held to be unstable when there is recurrent cardiac pain at rest that is more frequent, more prolonged, and more intense than usual. It is usually accompanied by ECG changes, but without cardiac enzyme release. Others will define unstable angina as the recent onset of cardiac pain which was previously stable, and which is now precipitated by minimal activity. Unstable cardiac pain is relatively common, and many centres report that unstable angina is a more common presenting diagnosis than evolving myocardial infarction.

Between 7 per cent and 22 per cent of patients with unstable angina proceed to develop acute myocardial infarction, and the one-year mortality is high, and can reach 20 per cent (Fulton *et al*. 1972; Gazes *et al*. 1973; Mulcahy *et al*. 1985). Those patients whose symptoms do not settle on medical treatment within 48 hours represent a particularly high-risk group (Roberts *et al*. 1983). De Servi *et al*. (1989) reported that in a multivariate analysis only three independent variables were predictive of poor prognosis: left main stem disease, three-vessel coronary disease, and elevated left ventricular end-diastolic pressure. Patients with all these variables had a 58 per cent three-year survival rate; those without any of these had a 98 per cent rate of survival. With the recognition of the benefit of antithrombotic therapy these event rates have fallen; but the need for revascularization procedures is high in this group, because of the development of further ischaemic cardiac pain.

Mechanism

The mechanism for the development of unstable cardiac pain appears to be the rupturing of an atheromatous plaque followed by platelet activation and thrombus formation. Under certain conditions coronary spasm can also contribute to the ischaemic process. Evidence for platelet activation and thromboxane A_2 production's being closely related to the timing of episodes of ischaemia occurring at rest is persuasive. As thromboxane A_2 is a powerful vasoconstrictor it is possible that it either precipitates or sustains the vasospasm occurring in unstable angina. Higher levels of fibrinogen have been identified in patients with unstable angina and non-Q wave infarction as compared with control subjects, and this increase was aggravated in smokers. It was not certain whether the increase in fibrinogen occurred as a cause or as a result of myocardial necrosis (Swahn *et al.* 1989).

Complex coronary arterial morphology is a common finding in patients with unstable angina. Approximately two-thirds of patients will have complex morphology or an intraluminal filling defect compatible with thrombus in the ischaemia-related artery. Unstable angina appears to be associated with transient reduction in coronary flow rather than with an increase in myocardial oxygen demand. Thallium scanning often shows a temporary defect of myocardial perfusion associated with ST depression and occurring at the time of ischaemia, suggesting that it is a reduction in flow which is the underlying cause.

SYNDROME X

This condition is characterized by typical cardiac pain in patients with normal coronary arteries (in whom coronary spasm cannot be demonstrated), who have objective evidence of transient cardiac ischaemia. The prognosis is usually good, and it has been suggested that the mechanism involved is a generalized flow-limiting abnormality of the smaller arterioles.

MANAGEMENT

Unstable angina is a potentially threatening condition which warrants early attention. Patients should be considered for hospital admission and placed on bed rest. Serial ECGs and enzymes should be monitored to identify myocardial infarction. It is probably reasonable to admit patients with unstable angina, and to a coronary care unit if possible. About 80 per cent of patients will respond to optimal medical therapy. Those who do not should undergo cardiac catheterization to stratify their risk and to see if a revascularization procedure is feasible.

Nitrates

Intravenous nitrates are established therapy for those patients who are able to tolerate nitrates, and in our institution we use intravenous GTN, which is cheaper than and as effective as isosorbide; the intravenous route is favoured because of the relative ease of titration compared with the oral formulations.

Dosage: 10–200 micrograms/minute according to clinical benefit and the effect on blood-pressure. An alternative is buccal GTN, which in doses of 5 mg six-hourly may be as successful as intravenous therapy, and obviates the need for an intravenous line and an infusion pump.

Aspirin

In the Veteran's Administration Cooperative Study (Lewis *et al.* 1983), patients with unstable angina receiving aspirin therapy had a 51 per cent reduction in mortality and acute myocardial infarction compared with patients receiving placebo. In the Canadian Multicentre Trial (Cairns *et al.* 1985) patients with unstable angina were randomized to aspirin, sulfinpyrazone, both drugs, or placebo: the incidence of sudden death over a two-year period was reduced by 51 per cent in patients receiving aspirin. Thus there is persuasive evidence for the use of aspirin in patients who have unstable cardiac pain.

Dosage: 150 mg per day, starting therapy at the earliest opportunity and administering the first dose either crushed or in soluble form to aid rapid absorption.

Heparin

Intravenous heparin has been shown to reduce the likelihood of progression of unstable angina to myocardial infarction (Telford and Wilson 1981).

Some centres employ both heparin and aspirin in the management of unstable angina. Support for this policy is provided by Wallentin *et al.* (1989), who found in a study of 800 patients with unstable angina or non-Q wave infarction that, in patients receiving a combination of aspirin plus five days' intravenous heparin, there was a lower rate of infarction and cardiac death than in patients receiving aspirin alone or placebo.

Beta-blockers and calcium-channel blockers

The addition of nifedipine to nitrates and a beta-blocker has been demonstrated to significantly reduce sudden death, myocardial infarction, and persistent angina requiring surgery (Gerstenblith *et al.* 1982). Presumably the mechanism of benefit may relate to reversal of coronary arterial spasm as a result of the vasodilating properties of calcium antagonism.

Other interventions

A minority of patients will continue to experience cardiac pain despite optimal medical therapy. These patients should be considered for revascularization with either angioplasty or coronary surgery.

The insertion of the intra-aortic balloon-assist device (see **procedures**, Chapter 8) is very likely to achieve relief of symptoms as a result of the afterload reduction and increased coronary diastolic flow that occurs with this technique. Such support does allow more protected cardiac catheterization, and buys time whilst this and possible revascularization are being arranged.

Despite the likely role of thrombosis in the mechanism of unstable cardiac pain, thrombolysis has not been shown to impact favourably in this situation, and in view of the potential for harm with these agents they should be withheld. They should of course be used promptly if an unstable patient should experience cardiac pain suggestive of infarction accompanied by evolving ECG changes; and, since many of these patients will be either in hospital or in the vicinity of medical assistance, in these cases thrombolysis is likely to be administered early, with considerable likelihood of myocardial salvage.

The Veteran's Administration Cooperative Study on Unstable Angina (Luchi *et al.* 1987) showed that, at two years' follow-up, 34 per cent of patients randomized to chronic medical therapy developed refractory, recurrent symptoms, and crossed over to surgical treatment. A follow-up report (Scott *et al.* 1988) has shown that, although overall survival figures show no significant difference between surgical and medical treatment, patients with impaired left ventricular function (ejection fractions of 30–49 per cent) had a significantly better survival when managed surgically than when treated medically. This is the first trial to show improved survival for patients with unstable angina managed surgically.

SILENT MYOCARDIAL ISCHAEMIA

It is increasingly recognized that some myocardial ischaemia occurs in the absence of symptoms. We know that many patients who die from ischaemic heart disease were asymptomatic with unsuspected coronary heart disease prior to their fatal event. Furthermore, 25 per cent of myocardial infarction is unrecognized clinically, and almost half these events are truly silent (Kannel and Abbott 1984). Silent ischaemia can be detected by stress-testing procedures, such as treadmill exercise and thallium perfusion imaging, being manifested as typical ischaemic changes in the absence of cardiac symptoms. However, much interest has centred on the role of ambulatory ECG monitoring. These monitors need to have adequate low-frequency response, as provided by frequency-modulated recorders. ST-segment shift identified in this way has been shown to be due to myocardial ischaemia by performing direct comparison studies with radioisotope imaging using rubidium 82 as a marker of myocardial perfusion (Deanfield *et al.* 1983).

ST-segment shift does occur in significant numbers of asymptomatic, healthy people, and a diagnosis of silent ischaemia should be reserved for episodes of asymptomatic ST depression occurring in patients with proven ischaemic heart disease who do not have left-bundle branch-block, left ventricular hypertrophy, or pre-excitation, or who are taking digoxin, all of which may give rise to false-positive ST change. Possible mechanisms for silent ischaemia include altered coronary tone and increased platelet aggregability. However, there continues to be controversy concerning the pathophysiology, and it may be that the role of altered coronary tone has been exaggerated hitherto: it seems likely that increase in myocardial oxygen demand contributes significantly in silent ischaemic events and the finding that beta-blockers are more effective in the treatment of asymptomatic ischaemic events than nitrates or calcium-blockers lends support to this. It seems that, in patients with ischaemic heart disease, the majority of ischaemic episodes are silent, as identified by ambulatory monitoring (Deanfield *et al.* 1983). Furthermore, in patients with unstable angina on optimal therapy transient ischaemic episodes are frequent, and a considerable majority of them are asymptomatic (Gottlieb *et al.* 1986).

In managing ischaemic heart disease, therefore, we should consider the total ischaemic burden, the combination of both the symptomatic and asymptomatic ischaemia (Cohn 1987).

Interestingly, it does seem that these episodes of silent ischaemia are more likely to occur during low levels of activity, and especially during periods of rest and sleep rather than during exercise. There appears to be a peak in the incidence of both silent and symptomatic ischaemia in the early morning, which parallels the increased rate of myocardial infarction and sudden death known to occur at this time of day.

Prognosis

The prognostic significance of silent ischaemia remains uncertain, but some information is available in this regard: we know from the Framingham Study that the 10-year survival of patients with unrecognized or silent infarction was similar to that of patients with symptomatic events (Kannel and Abbott 1984). Weiner *et al.* (1987), reporting from the Coronary Artery Surgery Study (CASS) registry of patients with stable coronary disease, have shown that about 27 per cent developed ST depression on exercise without angina. There was a 76 per cent seven-year survival in this group. In the 29 per cent of patients with both angina and ST depression the survival was similar, at 78 per cent. In those patients with coronary disease but neither ST depression or angina on exercise the seven-year survival was 88 per cent. In unstable angina, Gottlieb *et al.* (1986) found that 37 of 70 patients had episodes of transient ischaemia, 90 per cent of which were silent. These patients had a significantly higher possibility of an unfavourable outcome—either myocardial infarction or the need for a revascularization procedure—than those patients without silent ischaemic episodes.

AORTIC DISSECTION

Aortic dissection may mimic myocardial infarction closely, though the management of these conditions is quite different. It should be suspected in patients presenting with the sudden onset of usually severe pain, and may be accompanied by loss of pulses, aortic regurgitation, or the appearance of blood in the pleural or pericardial spaces. Dissection into a coronary may lead to myocardial infarction in addition. An attempt must be made to keep blood-pressure low (an infusion of labetalol in the dose range 125 micrograms to 2 mg/minute is useful in this regard) to prevent extension of the dissection, and a systolic pressure of 100 mm Hg is a reasonable aim. Echocardiography may support the diagnosis (transoesophageal imaging is especially useful), while a CT scan and/or angiography may be required to confirm the diagnosis. Surgery should be considered, and indeed a cardiovascular surgeon should be consulted soon after the diagnosis is established so that a co-ordinated plan can be formulated. These patients should not of course receive thrombolysis or anticoagulation.

4

Pre-hospital management

WHY WE SHOULD PROVIDE PRE-HOSPITAL CORONARY CARE

Patients begin to die early and unpredictably after myocardial infarction; about two-thirds of the deaths associated with myocardial infarction take place out of hospital, and 50 per cent of the patients who will die do so within two hours of the onset of symptoms, mostly as a result of ventricular fibrillation. All patients with chest pain suggestive of a cardiac origin of 20 minutes' or more duration, unrelieved by rest or nitrates, should at least be considered for prompt admission. Those patients who present later than 12 hours after infarction have less to gain from CCU admission, although admission to a medical ward will often be required.

Out-of-hospital mortality is increased if acute coronary care is delayed: in a study of two similar communities in Northern Ireland Mathewson *et al.* (1985) showed that the community served by a mobile coronary care facility had a lower mortality. The treatment in the two areas differed only in that it was delivered two hours earlier where mobile care was available. Sixty-three lives were estimated to have been saved by the provision of earlier care in this study: interestingly, only 5 per cent of these were accounted for by resuscitation from out-of-hospital ventricular fibrillation. A likely conclusion must be that it was the early and skilled provision of the management of pain, cardiac failure, and rhythm disturbance which resulted in this salvage.

Delay is contributed to by patients, by general practitioners, and by transport, and there is also in-hospital delay, giving rise to a median of four hours delay from the onset of infarct pain to arrival in coronary units in the United Kingdom. Since the majority of deaths after infarction occur within 2 hours, considerable potential exists for successful out-of-hospital rescue.

WHY THE DELAY?

While there are several factors contributing to the delay in patients' presenting for coronary care, the longest delay results from the interval between the onset of symptoms and the patient or spouse's calling for assistance, a median of two hours (Rawles and Haites 1988). This study also suggested that patients presenting early (within one hour) after the onset of symptoms had a mortality which was three times higher than in patients presenting at two to four hours. The authors conclude that the length of time that infarct pain is tolerated may be inversely related to the size of the infarction, which is itself the main determinant of mortality. The findings suggest that the patients' call for help and the doctors' response may be at an instinctive level according to the patients' distress; these patterns of behaviour may be difficult to modify by public education.

In a report from the British Heart Foundation Working Group (1989) the authors state:

'If the general practitioner is to play a part in managing patients with acute myocardial infarction it is essential that the practice is organised to allow a rapid response. Where it is feasible the best system is one in which the general practitioner and the ambulance service respond without delay, with the general practitioner contributing personal knowledge of the patient, diagnostic skill and pain relief with opiates and the ambulance service contributing resuscitation facilities and rapid transport'.

However, the authors of a report from the Nottingham Heart Attack Register suggest that their evidence supports a policy of rapid admission to hospital rather than out-of-hospital administration of thrombolysis in the urban environment (Rowley *et al.* 1992): in this report of 6712 patients admitted to hospital with suspected myocardial infarction, the median delay from onset of symptoms to hospital admission was 174 minutes, and the only factor that seemed to affect the time taken was the patient's decision to call a general practitioner or an ambulance: if a general practitioner was summoned the median delay was prolonged, at 247 minutes, compared with 100 minutes when an ambulance was summoned by the patient. The median time from the call for ambulance assistance to hospital arrival was 29 minutes. This study appears to overlook the well-described in-hospital delay before therapy is administered. It is accepted that there is no point in summoning a general practitioner in a case of suspected myocardial infarction if all that results is a call to the ambulance service: however, if earlier out-of-hospital coronary care is provided, with adequate analgesia, thrombolysis, and resuscitation where it is appropriate, then there is clear potential for mortality reduction, as has been demonstrated in the GREAT and EMIP studies, albeit in the treatment of patients at some distance from the hospital (GREAT Study Group 1992; EMIP Investigators 1992).

Burns *et al.* (1989) have reported that at their institution they were able to achieve a mean reduction of 51 minutes in the delay of admission of patients to the CCU by installing a direct telephone link to the CCU, bypassing the hospital switchboard, with the ambulance service's being made aware of a direct admission policy; this also resulted in a significant increase in the uptake of thrombolysis. They also reported no appreciable problems associated with congestion in the CCU or difficulty in transferring patients at an early stage to general wards if required.

SUDDEN DEATH

This is defined as death which is unexpected and which occurs without symptoms or within one hour of the onset of symptoms. It is the commonest mode of death in patients aged 20–64 years. The mechanism of death is likely to be arrhythmic, and therefore due to ventricular fibrillation and potentially reversible. In 75 per cent of cases there will be significant coronary disease, but only a minority will have experienced a myocardial infarction. The potential exists, therefore, for a favourable prognosis, provided of course that these patients are resuscitated from their threatening arrhythmia. This represents a significant problem, with sudden death accounting for 20 per cent of all natural mortality. The problem relates to the fact that mostly cardiac arrest is unexpected and unpredictable; and although immediate expert resuscitation might be life-saving for these patients, it is usually unavailable.

OUT-OF-HOSPITAL CARDIAC ARREST

There is evidence to show that impressive numbers of these patients can be saved by trained personnel: in Seattle, using paramedics combined with a training programme for citizens, 35 per cent of sudden-death patients are resuscitated initially by bystanders. Successful resuscitation is performed in about 60 per cent of cases, with 30 per cent being discharged home (Thompson *et al.* 1979). However, others have reported, also from the United States, that rates of successful, community resuscitation average 20 per cent, with even fewer surviving until hospital discharge (Gray *et al.* 1991).

Whether patients experiencing sudden death out of hospital will be successfully resuscitated depends on several factors: success is unlikely if the patient is not in ventricular fibrillation but in asystole, or has electromechanical dissociation (preserved electrical rhythm, but pulseless). Pulseless rhythms are likely to be associated with threatening cardiac conditions that are unlikely to be reversible, such as cardiac rupture or massive pulmonary embolism. A futher unfavourable factor is for the arrest to occur in the absence of a witness, which presumably affects the delay time between the onset of arrest and the start of effective resuscitation. Asystole is often the discovered arrhythmia in patients who experience an unwitnessed arrest, and is likely to have developed from untreated ventricular fibrillation.

It has been reported, following an analysis of the medical records of 296 people dying out of hospital of acute ischaemic heart disease, that since 91 per cent of people were dead before a call for help was made, there was little potential for significant impact on deaths outside hospital (Fitzpatrick *et al.* 1992): 73 per cent of the deaths occurred at home, and 40 per cent of the deaths were unwitnessed; therefore these people could not have received resuscitation. Only 16 per cent of the witnesses of a death attempted cardiopulmonary resuscitation before the arrival of a doctor or ambulance crew. In over half the cases in which resuscitation could have been attempted (but was not) death occurred in the presence of a spouse or close relative. Death occurred in the presence of a doctor or paramedic in a maximum of only 5 per cent of deaths outside hospital. The authors concluded that unless a greater proportion of patients receive cardiopulmonary resuscitation before emergency staff arrive, the provision of defibrillators to emergency staff is unlikely to have a significant impact on out-of-hospital deaths.

Continued resuscitation efforts in hospital emergency departments for those who have not responded to out-of-hospital resuscitation with advanced cardiac life-support is not recommended: they have not been shown to be worth while, consuming precious institutional and economic resources without gain (Gray *et al.* 1991). In this study, over a

19-month period, 16 of 185 patients (9 per cent) were successfully resuscitated in the hospital emergency department and admitted to hospital; all but one were comatose throughout their hospital stay, and none survived to leave hospital. The mean hospital stay was 12.6 days (range 11–32), with an average of 2.3 days in an intensive care unit, range 1–11 days. Defibrillation is the pivotal intervention for the management of ventricular fibrillation: medical therapy has not been shown persuasively to improve the rates of survival during cardiac arrest procedures. In fact one study has shown that medical therapy given initially resulted only in delaying defibrillation, and resulted in lower rates of survival (Weaver *et al.* 1990).

There is a clear attraction, therefore, to providing coronary care earlier, and therefore in the community. Pai *et al.* (1987) reported the experience of 1011 heart attacks in patients under the care of practitioners who practised cardiopulmonary resuscitation and were equipped with defibrillators. The general practitioner was the first medical contact in 92 per cent of heart attacks, and was equipped with a defibrillator in 80 per cent of such calls. Fifty-six patients had a cardiac arrest in the presence of the practitioner, and resuscitation was attempted in 47 cases, this being 5 per cent of all heart attack calls. Twenty-one (45 per cent) of resuscitated patients survived to reach hospital, and 13 (28 per cent) survived to leave hospital. The authors concluded that the opportunity for cardiopulmonary resuscitation in general practice occurs sufficiently often to justify the training and equipping of community doctors for advanced life-support. The same authors have calculated that a practice with 10 000 patients might expect to deal each year with 35 heart attacks, with one or two attempts at cardiac resuscitation. One doctor in such a practice may carry out resuscitation once every second year, with a successful outcome three or four times in a professional lifetime. There can be few occasions in a practitioner's career when he or she can be certain that his or her intervention has unquestionably saved a patient's life: resuscitation from cardiac arrest is one of those situations. The reward and clinical satisfaction resulting from such an experience can readily be imagined.

AUTOMATED DEFIBRILLATION

The development of the automated external defibrillator represents an important advance: this device recognizes and is able to defibrillate automatically patients who are in ventricular fibrillation, and many first-line paramedical services are being equipped with this device with benefit.

Dickey *et al.* (1992) have reported a sensitivity of 92.5 per cent for the correct identification of VF using a semi-automatic defibrillator, and a specificity of 94 per cent. In this study, the accuracy of decision-making of a semi-automatic defibrillator was assessed in 57 cardiac arrests: the authors concluded that the detection of cardiac rhythms using a microprocessor-based system for patients with cardiac arrest has a high sensitivity for VF and a high specificity for non-VF.

Cobbe *et al.* (1991) have reported the initial experience of the provision of automated defibrillators in Scottish front-line ambulances. During the study period 268 defibrillators were purchased by public subscription, and 96 per cent of 2000 ambulance crew underwent an eight-hour training programme in cardiopulmonary resuscitation and defibrillation. A total of 1111 cardiac arrests were recorded, and defibrillation was indicated and performed in 54 per cent of patients, who had a mean age of 63 years. A spontaneous pulse was present on arrival in hospital in 30 per cent of the defibrillated patients, and 12.5 per cent were subsequently discharged alive. The likelihood of survival was inversely related to the delay from onset of arrest to the time of first shock, and was greater in the case of a witnessed event: if the arrest occurred after the arrival of the ambulance, survival to discharge was 33 per cent. The authors concluded that an effective scheme for out-of-hospital defibrillation could be introduced rapidly and with limited training implications and costs, using automated defibrillators in ambulances.

These resuscitated patients remain at significant risk, with a one-year mortality of 26 per cent, mostly due to further cardiac arrest. This suggests that these patients require extensive in-hospital evaluation, including coronary arteriography and possibly electrophysiology, to stratify their risk and so that steps can be taken to reduce this threat with pharmacology or surgery, or by the insertion of an implantable defibrillator.

MYOCARDIAL INFARCTION

Premonitory symptoms of myocardial infarction are unreliable, and may be similar to those of angina. Indeed infarcts may be silent or may present with non-specific symptoms, such as nausea, weakness, sweating, or dyspnoea. However, the chest pain is more typically a crushing, constricting, choking sensation. It is usually substernal, but may radiate, as with angina, to the throat and jaw, to the left and right arms, and to the back. Similarly, signs are variably present, and include: an ill appearance; coldness/clamminess to palpation; sweating; a third or fourth heart sound; and arrhythmias.

The differential diagnosis is from among: pericarditis, pulmonary embolism, dissecting aneurysm, hiatus hernia, cervical spondylosis, and pneumothorax. Less likely, but possible, alternative diagnoses include pancreatitis, cholelithiasis, and intra-abdominal perforation.

Management of myocardial infarction

The electrocardiogram

Resting 12-lead electrocardiograms may be helpful for those who can interpret them, but can be normal in early infarction in 30 per cent of those shown subsequently to have myocardial infarction. If myocardial infarction is suspected but the presenting ECG is normal or equivocal, the tracing should be repeated 15 minutes later, and as frequently as is clinically appropriate. There is some evidence to suggest, however, that infarcting patients presenting with normal electrocardiograms are at reduced risk (ASSET Study Group 1988). Commonly seen ECG patterns are shown in Chapter 5—**hospital management of myocardial infarction**.

Admission of patients within 6 hours of the onset of infarct pain allows them to be considered for thrombolysis, which is of proven value in the salvage of myocardium and the reduction of mortality. Removal of a patient to a coronary care unit allows monitoring for threatening arrhythmias and prompt treatment during the time when the ischaemic ventricle is at its most unstable electrically.

Although some flexibility should be employed, it is likely that patients presenting within 12 hours of infarction will derive optimum benefit from coronary care management.

Clearly the majority of patients admitted to the unit will have chest pain syndromes and be suspected of having acute myocardial infarction: most units, however, will admit patients with other threatening cardiac conditions for observation and management, and these will include serious arrhythmias and patients with advanced cardiac failure requiring haemodynamic monitoring.

THE ROLE OF THE GENERAL PRACTITIONER

Clearly the most appropriate and earliest coronary care can be provided by a well-equipped, dedicated, coronary ambulance manned by trained staff who are skilled in resuscitation and able to administer appropriate drugs. In the absence of such a service the role of a physician is to establish the diagnosis with a brief history and examination, employing a 12-lead ECG if it is available.

Rawles (1987) has reported the replies to a questionnaire sent to general practitioners who had previously participated in a study of pre-hospital cardiopulmonary resuscitation and defibrillation in acute myocardial infarction: only 16 of 50 respondents thought that every general practitioner should have a defibrillator, but 46 thought that every practice should have one. Most felt the need for more tuition and practice in advanced life-support; but 15 did not have the practice defibrillator with them whilst on call, and only nine had an ECG machine with them. Twenty-three said they would be prepared to use thrombolysis in the community.

In the same study the author reported that 33 of 50 respondents identified correctly a normal ECG, 37 an ECG showing acute myocardial infarction, 33 a tracing of left-bundle branch-block, and seven an ECG showing acute pericarditis. Clearly some of the practitioners, despite contributing earlier to a study of pre-hospital resuscitation, were less well able to cope with an arrest, being unaccompanied by a defibrillator whilst on call.

Davies (1989) reports that a substantial minority of general practitioners do not have access to an electrocardiograph, and a majority do not use them when faced with a patient with acute myocardial infarction. This despite the fact that there will be approximately 100 consultations for chest pain per year in a practice with a list size of 2500; the average general practice is likely to see about 10 patients per year with acute myocardial infarction. He further points out that these machines are reasonably priced at about £1200 (1989 prices), and are tax-allowable and have low revenue implications. He concludes that all general practitioners should aspire to own, and to be able to use, an electrocardiograph.

Colquhoun (1988) has reported the one-year experience of 49 practices who had been donated defibrillators by the British Heart Foundation. Twenty-five practices (99 doctors) recorded the use of the defibrillator, and 24 practices (100 doctors) recorded no use during the study period. Fifty-three attempts at resuscitation were made; 16 (30 per cent) reached hospital alive, 10 (19 per cent) surviving to leave hospital. Success was highest when ventricular fibrillation was the underlying rhythm disturbance (32 patients), with 12 (37 per cent) reaching hospital alive and 7 (22 per cent) being discharged alive. The estimated time to reaching patients in ventricular fibrillation was 4.8 minutes. Nineteen patients experienced arrest in the presence or immediate vicinity of a general practitioner; in this group the initial success rate was 68 per cent, with 47 per cent surviving to leave hospital. In summary, the 25 defibrillators used in the first year after their availability to general practitioners saved 10 lives.

The same author (Colquhoun 1989) subsequently reported the results of a further postal study of 348 general practitioners in 90 practices, among whom responses were received from 91 per cent of the practices and 88 per cent of the doctors. In total 62 per cent of the doctors had access to an ECG machine, 45 per cent of them recording a tracing in suspected myocardial infarction during surgery hours, and 26 per cent doing so outside working hours. When those doctors not owning an ECG machine were included, 28 per cent of doctors recorded a tracing during surgery hours and 16 per cent outside normal working hours; only 13 per cent routinely carried an ECG machine with them outside normal working hours. The author concludes that if the administration of thrombolysis was contingent on the confirmation of infarction by electrocardiography, the widespread introduction of these agents was likely to be delayed.

There is now the possibility of transmitting ECG information by cellular telephone: this would allow paramedics or practitioners in-experienced in ECG interpretation to receive guidance in this regard from a cardiac centre. In Seattle, where this system is operating, the reported rate of transmission failure is 8 per cent (Califf and Harrelson-Woodlief 1990).

ANALGESIA

Analgesia should be administered promptly, since anxiety and pain increase myocardial oxygen demand, which is undesirable in this situation. Furthermore, the release of excess catecholamines may allow the development of threatening arrhythmias. Opiates exert favourable effects by being analgesic and anxiolytic, and they have desirable vasodilatory properties in addition, whereby they reduce pulmonary congestion.

- **Diamorphine** 2.5−5.0 mg should be used intravenously at 1 mg/minute, in addition to increments of 2.5 mg at 10-minute intervals until pain is relieved.

The opiates may result in hypotension because of their vasodilatory effects, and they may also be associated with respiratory depression, especially in patients with airways disease, in whom a smaller dose should be administered in small increments. Any respiratory depression may be reversed with naloxone (0.8 mg intravenously); and this may need to be repeated at intervals of two minutes to a maximum 10 mg, remembering that the analgesic effects of the opiate will also be reversed.

- **Pentazocine** should be *avoided* as an analgesic in this situation, as it increases left ventricular pre- and afterload, which is undesirable.

- **Cyclizine** 50 mg should be used to limit the associated nausea of the opiate, and both should be given intravenously, to achieve a rapid and reliable response, but also to reduce the possibility of confounding enzyme release from skeletal muscle's interfering with the subsequent diagnosis.

- **Metoclopramide** 10 mg should be used in the presence of shock or left ventricular failure, to avoid the potential constrictor properties of cyclizine.

Other interventions

If there is no contraindication to its use, soluble aspirin 150 mg should be administered at the earliest opportunity.

If available, oxygen should be employed, and arrangements should be made to transfer the patient to a coronary care unit as soon as possible. The need for early transfer should not mean the neglect of the management of infarct complications, however; and whenever possible appropriate analgesia should be provided, and a practitioner or skilled paramedic should remain with the patient, who should ideally be attached to a monitor, with a defibrillator available.

If time allows an intravenous cannula should be inserted into an arm vein to allow administration of intravenous therapy; the insertion of such a device at the time of a cardiac arrest is necessarily much more difficult. It can prove helpful if at the time of cannula-insertion a 10 ml venous blood sample is taken, labelled, and sent in with the patient; if, subsequently, defibrillation is performed any hospital-obtained samples will be difficult to interpret, in view of the skeletal muscle damage. Right-sided antecubital veins should be avoided whenever possible, so as to allow their use for insertion of haemodynamic catheters if these are needed.

THROMBOLYSIS

Following myocardial infarction the most important discriminator of long- and short-term morbidity and mortality is the amount of myocardium which remains viable. Studies have shown that significant amounts of myocardium can be salvaged by treatment with beta-blockade (ISIS-1 Collaborative Group 1988) and nitrates (Yusuf *et al.* 1988); but considerable evidence now exists for the role of early thrombolysis (GISSI Trial Study Group 1986; ISIS-2 Collaborative Group 1988).

Patients likely to have experienced an acute infarction should be considered for thrombolysis at the earliest opportunity after evaluation. The earlier the infarct-related artery is recanalized the more likely is the benefit. Every effort should be made to shorten the delay between presentation and administration of the thrombolytic agent.

Pre-hospital thrombolysis

Practitioners working in areas remote from coronary care units should consider administering thrombolysis in the community, in view of the potential for reducing mortality by up to 50 per cent with these agents and the decay of benefit if there are significant time-delays. Those working near to hospitals with coronary care units (and those without access to 12-lead ECG machines) are probably best advised to admit their patients with suspected myocardial infarction at the earliest possible time: this allows the decision concerning thrombolysis to be made in an environment where the expertise and equipment exists to facilitate decision-making, but also to deal with the consequences of this therapy.

The most convenient agent to use in the community is anistreplase, as it is administered as an intravenous bolus of 30 units over 3–5 minutes, the other thrombolytic agents requiring an infusion which is likely to be problematic during patient-transfer.

Studies have shown impressive savings in time-delay when thrombolysis is administered out of hospital (The Thrombolysis Early in Acute Heart Attack Study Group 1990). The European Myocardial Infarction Project (EMIP) has shown that pre-hospital treatment reduces delay to intervention by about one hour (EMIP Subcommittee 1988). In this study patient-selection was made by a fully-equipped, mobile coronary care team led by a physician. Patients presenting within six hours of the onset of typical symptoms of acute myocardial infarction with ECG changes suggestive of acute infarction were randomized to receive either anistreplase (APSAC) at home and a matching placebo after admission to hospital or a placebo first, followed by the same anistreplase regimen after admission.

The results of this study have now been reported to the American College of Cardiology: the authors report that treating heart-attack victims with a thrombolytic before they reach hospital, rather than waiting till they are admitted, can reduce cardiac deaths by 17 per cent (EMIP Investigators 1992). The median interval between pre-hospital and in-hospital treatment, which represents the real time gained by pre-hospital therapy, was 56 minutes. However, in this study the hospital 'door-to-needle time' was unusually low, at 15 minutes: most hospitals would experience a considerably longer hospital delay, with a consequently greater time-saving. The time gained in EMIP is likely therefore to have been a considerable underestimate of the potential gain in current clinical practice.

The accuracy of pre-hospital diagnosis was high; diagnosis was confirmed in 93 per cent of patients on admission, and in 94 per cent of all patients on discharge.

The incidence of stroke, severe bleeding, shock, ventricular fibrillation, and reinfarction was similar in the two groups. Ventricular fibrillation and shock was experienced by a small proportion of both the pre-hospital and in-hospital groups.

Overall, pre-hospital thrombolysis was associated with reductions in both total and cardiac mortality (13 per cent, $p = 0.1$; 17 per cent, $p = 0.04$ respectively). Total mortality was reduced most in those patients who had the longest transportation time: a 50 per cent reduction was observed in those patients who experienced delays greater than 60 minutes ($p < 0.0002$).

Information from the Grampian Region Early Anistreplase Trial (GREAT) suggests a median delay from onset of pain to delivery of thrombolysis by rural general practitioners of 101 minutes; this compares favourably with a median of 240 minutes from the onset of symptoms to the administration of therapy in hospital (GREAT Study Group 1992).

In this randomized double-blind trial patients suspected of having acute myocardial infarction received either anistreplase or placebo at home from their general practitioners. The alternative injection was administered later in hospital; the average distance of these rural practices from the coronary unit in Aberdeen was 59 km (range 26–100). Myocardial infarction was confirmed in 78 per cent.

Median intervals in minutes were: onset of symptoms to call for GP 45 (0–210); from call to arrival of GP 10 (0–80); from arrival of GP to home injection 43 (5–145); and from home injection to hospital injection 130 (40–370).

By three months after trial entry the relative reduction of deaths from all causes in patients given thrombolytic therapy at home was 49 per cent ($p = 0.04$). Also, full thickness Q wave infarction was less common in patients with confirmed infarction receiving treatment at home—a 14.6 per cent reduction ($p = 0.02$). Benefits were most marked when thrombolytic therapy was administered within two hours of the onset of symptoms. Thus the results of these two studies of pre-hospital thrombolysis are complimentary and suggest a substantial temporal and mortality advantage in pre-hospital administration of thrombolysis.

This and other pre-hospital therapy studies have compared out-of-hospital therapy with hospital CCU treatment: there are often considerable delays between hospital admission and the administration of thrombolysis (an estimated median of 87 minutes in the GREAT study). We should beware of considering that the hospital presentation to therapy time has been optimal, and there is clear potential for a 'fast track' system to shave valuable time off the hospital delay. Pell *et al.* (1992) have compared the delays in admission to hospital and administration of thrombolysis before and after introducing a fast-track system: patients fulfilling clinical and electrocardiographic criteria for myocardial infarction were selected for rapid access to the cardiac care team, bypassing evaluation by the medical registrar.The fast-track system correctly identified 62 per cent of the patients who subsequently required thrombolytic treatment. Ninety-five per cent of patients treated with thrombolysis after fast-track admission had the diagnosis confirmed by electrocardiographic and enzyme analysis. The median delay from hospital admission to thrombolytic therapy fell from 93 minutes to 49 minutes in fast-track patients ($p = 0.001$). Delay in admission to the cardiac care unit was reduced by 47 per cent for fast-track patients. The authors concluded that, without extra staff or equipment, the fast-track system halved in-hospital delay to thrombolytic therapy without affecting the accuracy of diagnosis among patients requiring thrombolysis.

Possible adverse effects of thrombolysis

The potential risks of thrombolytic therapy should be understood, so that an early decision can be made concerning the risk—benefit ratio of thrombolytic therapy.

Many practitioners will have concern about the possibility of adverse effects resulting from the use of pre-hospital thrombolysis: clearly the development of stroke is the most important possible adverse effect, as it is usually associated with devastating consequences for the patient. Studies suggest that the incidence of cerebral haemorrhage is of the order of 0.5 per cent (5 per thousand patients treated). However, the total incidence of stroke is not increased, since although there is an increased rate of cerebral haemorrhage there is also a reduction in thrombotic stroke: thus there may be no excess of stroke associated with thrombolysis. Serious adverse effects otherwise appear to be uncommon, with the major mortality studies suggesting a reduced frequency of major cardiovascular complications, including cardiogenic shock, in thrombolysed patients (ISIS-2 Collaborative Group 1988).

Haemorrhage occurring during transport to hospital has not been reported, nor has stroke following thrombolytic therapy prior to hospital admission.

During pre-hospital evaluation, false-positive diagnoses of myocardial infarction occur infrequently: out of 155 diagnoses of acute myocardial infarction, Castaigne and colleagues reported only six false positives in a study involving junior anaesthetists and mobile coronary care units (Castaigne *et al.* 1989). No false-positive diagnoses were reported in a study of 110 patients treated by emergency care doctors in Germany (Kokott *et al.* 1990). These studies involved specialist teams and electrocardiograms were available, so these findings should not be assumed to apply in different circumstances; but in the GREAT study (where the pre-hospital randomization did not depend on the ECG), the diagnosis of infarction was confirmed in 78 per cent of patients.

Another concern relates to the possibility of reperfusion arrhythmias following treatment: McNeill *et al.* (1989) have reported that ventricular fibrillation was no more common in patients receiving thrombolysis than was seen in an earlier study of acute myocardial infarction without thrombolysis.

Important adverse effects within the first hour after therapy are unusual, and it has been reported that there is no difference in the frequency of complications during transportation whether the patient did or did not receive pre-hospital thrombolysis (Roth *et al.* 1990). With pre-hospital treatment ventricular fibrillation occurred in 2.7 per cent, compared with 4.5 per cent who did not receive pre-hospital thrombolysis. In a review of the role of pre-hospital thrombolysis, Wilcox (1990) stated that 'thrombolytic treatment could and should be given out of hospital after a careful evaluation of the patient, particularly if undue delay in transport to hospital is expected'. Furthermore, 'General practitioners should expect guidance and support from their local cardiovascular physician and proffer their collaboration in trials of thrombolytic therapy outside hospital'.

When should thrombolysis be used?

Currently my advice is to administer a thrombolytic within six hours of the patient's last pain, or later if the patient is still experiencing cardiac pain and therefore possibly still infarcting. The EMERAS study has shown that patients randomized to streptokinase more than six hours after infarction do not have a significantly improved survival compared with placebo: we should however apply a degree of flexibility here, as it is difficult to establish the exact timing of the onset of infarction, and we should attempt to avoid withholding potential benefit (see late study, page 65).

The evidence, however, supports using a 12-lead ECG to guide therapy in order to optimize benefit from therapy while limiting adverse effects. Additionally, an early ECG documents arrhythmias and ischaemic changes which may be short-lived, and therefore constitutes valuable evidence to be sent into hospital with the patient. We should not administer thrombolysis to those with normal ECGs, since their risk, even if they are shown subsequently to have infarcted, is lower, and the adverse effects may then outweigh the benefit. In addition, age is not a contraindication to thrombolysis: as the relative benefit of treatment is similar, the absolute benefit is considerable, in view of the excess mortality from infarction in the elderly.

We can conclude that patients within six hours of a likely infarction with ST elevation or left-bundle branch-block should be evaluated for thrombolysis irrespective of age. If there is likely to be a delay in admitting the patient out-of-hospital thrombolysis should be an available option. All patients should receive aspirin in a dose of 150 mg as soon as possible (either crushed or in soluble form to aid absorption).

If the patient has received streptokinase (or anistreplase) more than four days previously this should probably not be readministered, because of the potential of antistreptokinase and neutralizing antibodies to inhibit clot lysis and cause hypersensitivity (Lee *et al.* 1992*a*).

A more extensive review of thrombolysis is presented in **hospital management** (Chapter 5).

CARDIAC ARREST

Cardiac arrest should be assumed when:

- there is sudden, unexplained collapse;
- a seizure occurs in a patient at risk of cardiac arrest; or
- there is the sudden development of cyanosis.

Other causes of collapse should be considered, however; and in particular a cerebrovascular event, hypoglycaemia, hypovolaemia, and vasovagal syncope are potential causes.

A rapid assessment of the patient will establish whether there is spontaneous breathing and a pulse, and prompt cardiopulmonary resuscitation should be instituted if there is not. The time of starting resuscitation should be noted, and assistance should be summoned if it is available. Ventricular fibrillation is the usual terminal arrhythmia, and with early recognition and therapy many of these events can be reversed. The detailed management of cardiac arrest (and other adverse events) is described in **complications**, Chapter 6; but the technique relevant to out-of-hospital cardiac arrest is described here.

Basic life-support (the maintenance of an airway, the circulation, and breathing without the aid of specialized equipment), if performed well by trained personnel, can support life for an hour or more. Regular practice will be required, as these skills become blunted with time.

Out-of-hospital cardiac arrest procedure

- A: Airway
- B: Breathing
- C: Circulation

Airway

Once it is established that the patient is unconscious, the airway should be opened by lifting the chin forwards with one hand whilst pressing the forehead backwards, thereby clearing the airway. A quick pass of a finger around the inside of the mouth lessens the possibility of any material which might obstruct respiration.

If there is an assistant, the jaw should be supported forward by pushing upward on the angles of the mandible.

Breathing

With the ear placed close to the patient's mouth any spontaneous respiration can be seen by inspection of the chest and abdomen, and heard. If there is no spontaneous respiration, artificial respiration is provided by maintaining the airway, occluding the patient's nose, and breathing into the patient's mouth directly or through a face-mask with a one-way valve, which minimizes the infection risk.

Circulation

Check the pulse at the carotid artery: if the pulse is absent, with the patient on a flat, firm surface, place the heel of one hand just above the xiphisternum (Fig. 4.1). Place the other hand on top. With straight arms and standing as directly over the sternum as possible, vertically depress the sternum about 5 cm and release, repeating this process about 80 times per minute. Two respirations per 15 compressions should be made; but if assistance is available the ratio should be 5:1.

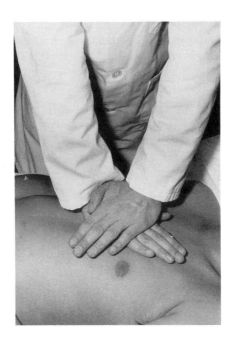

Fig. 4.1 Correct positioning of hands for external cardiac massage.

If an ECG tracing is available and shows:

● **Electromechanical dissociation** (QRS present but no pulse palpable): Give adrenaline 1 mg (10 ml of 1:10 000) intravenously, and consider the possibility of hypovolaemia, massive pulmonary embolism, or cardiac tamponade.

● **Asystole:** Give adrenaline 1 mg intravenously. If ventricular fibrillation results treat as described below under that heading. It is worth while cautioning that a straight line on the ECG may not reflect asystole, but equipment failure, or sometimes simply the disconnection of an ECG skin electrode.

● **Profound bradycardia:** Give atropine 600–1200 micrograms intravenously. Follow with adrenaline 1 mg if unsuccessful.

● **Ventricular fibrillation:** Immediate cardioversion is required. Conduction jelly (or preferably gel-impregnated pads) should be applied to the right of the upper half of the sternum and on the left chest as far laterally as possible (Fig. 4.2). Jelly must not be allowed to lie on the chest connecting the two areas, for fear of allowing arcing of energy during defibrillation. The paddles should be applied firmly to the chest wall, and attention must be given to ensuring that neither the operator or any assistant is touching the patient during electrical discharge.

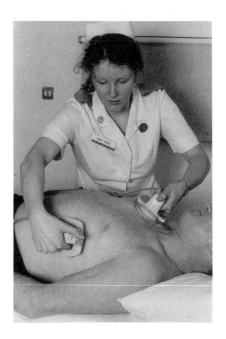

Fig. 4.2 Position of defibrillator paddles during cardioversion.

Cardioversion procedure

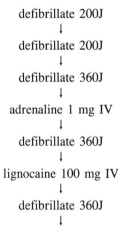

defibrillate 200J
↓
defibrillate 200J
↓
defibrillate 360J
↓
adrenaline 1 mg IV
↓
defibrillate 360J
↓
lignocaine 100 mg IV
↓
defibrillate 360J
↓

The high-energy defibrillation should be repeated until a decision is made to abandon the procedure.

Studies have shown that, for resuscitated patients, an arrest lasting more than 12–15 minutes is an independent predictor of death (Taffet *et al.* 1988; Cummins *et al.* 1985).

Chest compression should be continued for up to two minutes after each drug administration, and should not be interrupted for more than 10 seconds for any intervention.

If an intravenous line is not available, adrenaline, atropine, and lignocaine may be given down an endotracheal tube, if this has been inserted, in which case double the quoted doses should be employed. Intracardiac administration of drugs is unreliable and potentially hazardous, and should probably be reserved for experienced operators—and then when the clinical situation is bleak.

If the resuscitation is prolonged consider giving 50 mmol of sodium bicarbonate (50 ml of 8.4 per cent) but **never** down an endotracheal tube.

If an ECG is not available assume the patient is in ventricular fibrillation and proceed as above. Spontaneous patient movement and small pupils (if the patient has not received opiates), indicate delivery of oxygen to the brain, and are reassuring evidence of successful restoration of the circulation: dilated pupils do not necessarily connote a poor outcome, however.

Training

The Royal College of Physicians have reported that 220 out-of-hospital arrests would occur amongst half a million people each year, and that with paramedic units available 30—40 individuals could leave hospital alive. They comment that although the management of cardiopulmonary arrest is relatively simple, the availability and efficiency of resuscitative procedures are lacking in both the community and the hospital, owing mainly to inadequate training and organization. The College has made the following recommendations:

● All hospital staff should be trained in basic life-support, with extended training for doctors, qualified nurses, and ambulance personnel.

● In the community there should be regular training in basic life-support for dentists and the public at large, and extended training for general practitioners.

● Resuscitation skills should be tested in the professional qualifying and diploma examinations for doctors and nurses.

● Each district health authority and hospital should appoint a full-time resuscitation training officer, and the district and hospital should have a resuscitation committee responsible for overall management of procedures.

● Health authorities should provide all the necessary equipment and facilities for training (Royal College of Physicians 1987).

In 1986 a community resuscitation training programme was initiated at St Bartholemew's Hospital, intending to train one-third of the population of the City of London in life-saving techniques: this programme, which is funded entirely by donations, has trained thousands on a two-hour course dealing with the recognition of, and management of, cardiac arrest.

The British Association For Immediate Care (BASICS), a registered charity, consists of general practitioners who have formed an organization to provide a local immediate-care service, and who have provided themselves with the necessary equipment and training.

SUMMARY OF PRE-HOSPITAL CARE

1. Promptly establish diagnosis (history, examination, and ECG if available).
2. Administer appropriate analgesia and antiemetic.
3. Reduce anxiety in patient and relatives by calm, unemotive explanation of diagnosis and proposed plan.
4. Consider relative merits of administration of thrombolysis or prompt transfer to hospital with direct admission to the coronary care unit, bypassing accident and emergency departments.
5. Attempt to stay with patient, especially if defibrillator available, until the arrival of paramedical assistance with defibrillator capability.
6. Whenever possible the admitting ward and doctor should be made aware of the imminent arrival of a likely infarction patient. This limits the already considerable delays in early management inherent in the system.

THE CORONARY CARE UNIT

The development of coronary care units in the 1960s showed that sudden death was reversible; cardiac monitoring and prompt treatment of arrhythmias reduced the incidence of in-hospital mortality, and now it is cardiac failure and cardiogenic shock which are the commonest causes of death. So initially these units were appropriate environments to allow myocardial healing to take place; subsequently, they provided prophylaxis and management of arrhythmias; and now we have the exciting prospect of limiting infarct size and salvaging myocardium with thrombolysis, as a considerable majority of transmural infarctions are associated with coronary thrombosis (DeWood *et al.* 1980), in addition to providing early relief of symptoms and complications.

Coronary care units also allow useful risk-stratification to determine which patients require additional intervention; and we should not underestimate their role in training young doctors and nurses and in the performance of research.

Finally, it should be remembered that there is no ideal, inflexible, or routine therapy for patients with infarction; each patient's management needs should be assessed on an individual basis.

Suitable patients for admission to the coronary care unit

● Patients suspected of having experienced myocardial infarction less than 12 hours previously;

● patients with complications of myocardial infarction: arrhythmias, shock, and continuing cardiac pain; and

● patients with acute coronary insufficiency.

5

Hospital management of myocardial infarction

The immediate in-hospital management of myocardial infarction is necessarily similar to early coronary care in the community. Once again a prompt diagnosis is desirable, and patients should not be allowed to stack up unseen by a physician, in the mistaken belief that their being in hospital is sufficiently protective.

It is good medical practice for a doctor with a defibrillator and a monitor to accompany patients likely to be infarcting to the unit.

An attempt should be made to keep a bed free in the coronary unit at all times, and patients with presumed myocardial infarction or acute unstable cardiac pain should always be managed in a coronary care unit if possible.

THE ELECTROCARDIOGRAM

There is a likelihood of infarction in patients presenting with 20 minutes or more of cardiac-sounding pain unrelieved by nitrates and accompanied by ECG changes compatible with infarction. It should be remembered, however, that a significant minority of patients who present with minor ECG abnormalities will be shown to have experienced infarction on subsequent testing and on enzyme evidence.

In a review of 3697 patients presenting to coronary care units with 30 minutes or more of presumed cardiac pain, patients were assessed for ECG characteristics predictive of infarction: the abnormalities were: new Q waves (more than 30 ms wide and 0.2 mV deep) in at least two of leads 11, 111, or aVF, or in at least two of the six precordial leads (V_{1-6}), or in 1 and aVL; new ST segment elevation or depression of 0.1 mV or more in one of the same lead combinations; or complete left-bundle branch-block. The diagnostic sensitivity of these ECG criteria was 81 per cent, although the overall infarction rate in the screened population was 49 per cent. The diagnostic specificity was 69 per cent, and the predictive value was 72 per cent (Rude *et al.* 1983).

The admission ECG is a very useful tool in stratifying the risks of the patients, and therefore in deciding whether their management is best carried out in a coronary care unit or in a general ward, thereby releasing beds for patients at increased risk: a completely normal ECG makes infarction unlikely. About 60 per cent of patients with infarction will have acute evolving changes. The considerable majority of those without these changes but shown subsequently to have infarcted will have non-specific ECG changes. A study performed in our institution has shown that of 1200 consecutive patients with suspected acute myocardial infarction, only two patients with normal ECGs either died or experienced cardiac arrest. Admitting only those patients with infarct-sounding pain and abnormal ECGs to the coronary care unit would have meant only two of these at-risk patients' being managed on the general wards instead of in the coronary care unit, where their likelihood of survival is improved.

Lee *et al.* (1987) showed that only 4 per cent of infarction was misdiagnosed and discharged from the emergency ward, and that about half of these missed infarcts could have been diagnosed by improved ECG-reading skills.

We should always bear in mind, however, that the ECG is a relatively crude tool, and pseudoinfarct changes may be seen in highly trained athletes, in patients of African or West Indian origin, and in those with pre-excitation (WPW syndrome), hypertrophic cardiomyopathy, and subarachnoid haemorrhage.

ECG changes

The changes on the resting electrocardiogram in transmural myocardial infarction are as follows:

(a) There is ST elevation in the leads opposite the infarct zone.

(b) Q waves appear within a few hours, and are totally negative deflections of 0.04 of a second (one small square), or wider and/or deeper than 25 per cent of the R wave in the same lead.

(c) Subsequently the ST segment returns to baseline and the T wave inverts over a period of days.

(d) Persistent elevation of the ST segment may reflect the development of an aneurysm, and Q wave changes usually persist as a long-term legacy of the infarct; but a significant minority of electrocardiograms return to normal.

The myocardial territory in jeopardy can be localized using the electrocardiogram as follows:

Anterior infarction (Fig. 5.1)

Changes in leads V_1-V_4: anteroseptal infarction.
Changes in leads V_1-V_6: anterolateral infarction.

Inferior infarction (Fig. 5.2)

Changes in leads II, III, and aVF.

Posterior infarction (Fig. 5.3)

Tall R waves in leads V_1-V_2 (R wave taller than the S wave.)

Reciprocal ST change (Fig. 5.4)

The mechanism responsible for ST depression in leads remote from the infarct site (reciprocal ST change) is controversial; it is however associated with larger infarcts and more frequent complications. The finding of such ST depression may therefore act as a useful marker of increased patient risk (Jennings *et al.* 1983).

Left-bundle branch-block (Fig. 5.5)

In this conduction defect the QRS complexes are wider than 0.12 seconds (3 small squares), and this makes diagnosis more difficult unless this conduction defect has developed acutely, in which case it is compatible with infarction. Otherwise the finding of a Q wave in leads 1, aVL, and V_6 makes infarction likely.

Subendocardial infarction (or non-Q wave infarction) (Fig. 5.6)

Patients presenting with a history of infarct-sounding pain but who do not have Q waves but deep symmetrical T waves may have subendocardial infarction. These infarcts have been thought previously to be non-transmural, but it is now recognized that the ECG is too crude for any such anatomical discrimination. Furthermore, it should not be assumed that subendocardial infarction is associated with a more benign prognosis: in one study 21 per cent of these patients went on to develop full thickness infarction in one year (Madigan *et al.* 1976).

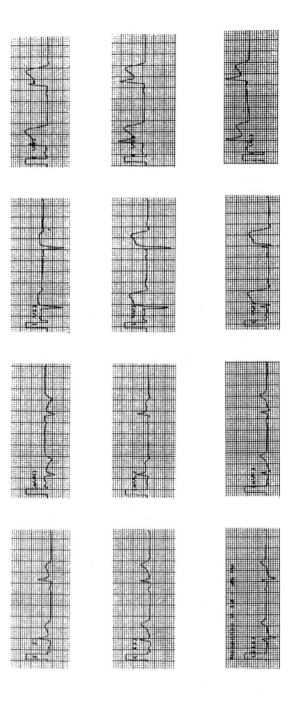

Fig. 5.1 Anterior myocardial infarction.

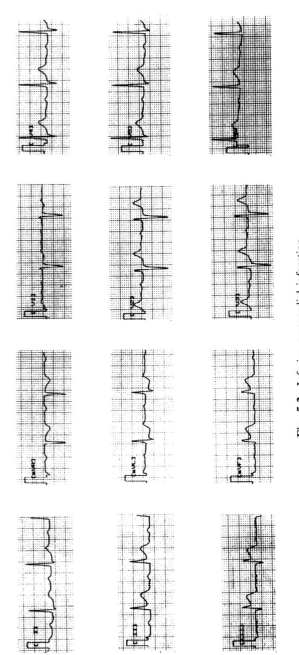

Fig. 5.2 Inferior myocardial infarction.

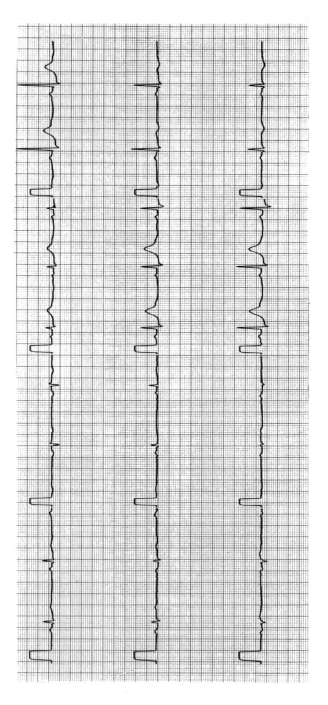

Fig. 5.3 Posterior myocardial infarction. Note the tall R waves in leads V_1 and V_2.

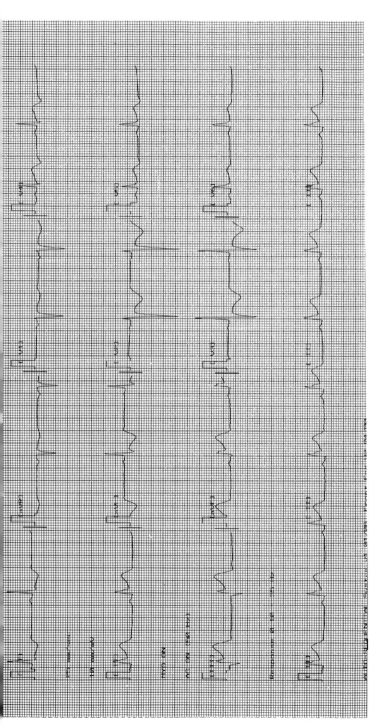

Fig. 5.4 Reciprocal ST depression. Note the ST depression in leads remote from the infarct site.

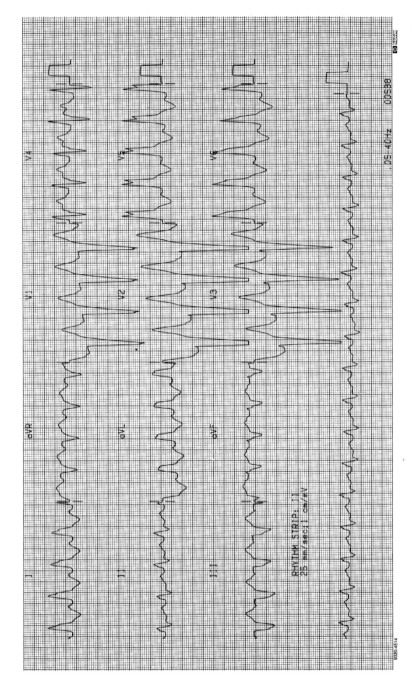

RHYTHM STRIP: II
25 mm/sec; 1 cm/mV

05-40Hz   00538

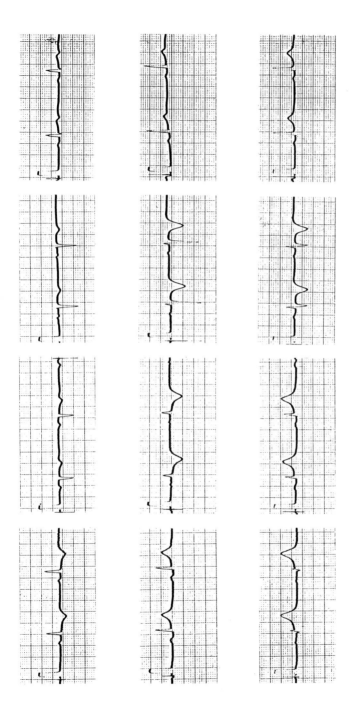

Fig. 5.6 Subendocardial (non-Q wave) myocardial infarction.

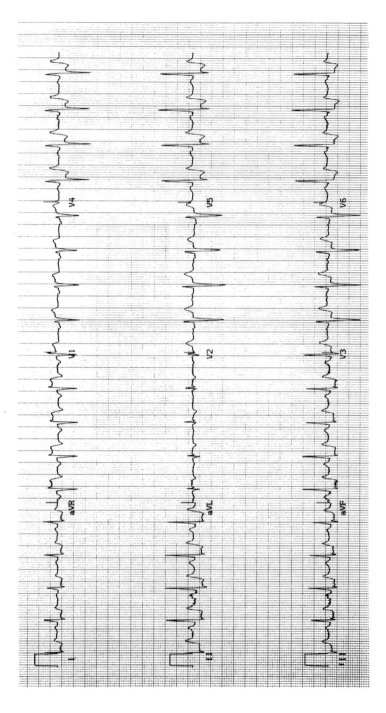

Fig. 5.7 ST depression in the inferolateral leads.

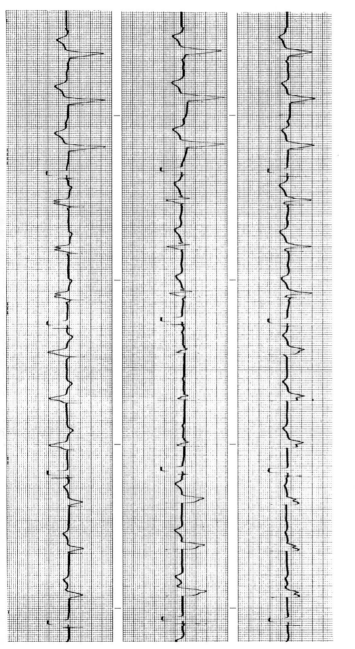

Fig. 5.8 Ventricular paced rhythm. Note the pacing spikes before each QRS complex.

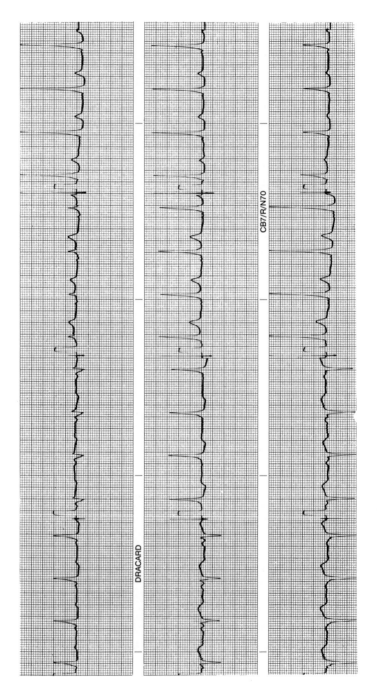

Fig. 5.9 Pre-excitation. Note the slurred QRS upstroke (delta wave) and short PR interval.

ST depression (Fig. 5.7)

Patients recruited into the ISIS-2 and GISSI trials who had ST depression on their presenting electrocardiogram had a high mortality of 16−19 per cent: this was not reduced by thrombolysis.

Lee *et al.* (1992*b*) reviewed a series of 136 patients suspected of having myocardial infarction, who only had ST depression on their presenting electrocardiogram: 74 (54 per cent) of these were subsequently confirmed to have experienced infarction on enzyme analysis. The nine-month mortality was 22 per cent for all patient groups and 28 per cent for those with confirmed infarction. The nine-month mortality was lower in patients showing only 1 mm of ST depression (11.1 per cent), or with 2 or less leads showing ST depression (7.1 per cent). It was higher in those with >2 mm ST depression (34.4 per cent), or with >3 leads showing ST depression (25.9 per cent). The electrocardiograms of those with infarction showed more ST depression, mean 2.5 mm, and more leads showed ST depression, mean 4.7 leads, when compared with those without infarction. For the subsequent diagnosis of myocardial infarction, ST depression of >4 mm was 20 per cent sensitive but 97 per cent specific. The sensitivity and specificity for ST depression occurring in >7 leads was 21 per cent and 95 per cent respectively.

The ECG and permanent pacing

In patients with a permanent pacing generator, the typical ECG changes of infarction will be hidden by the presence of wide, bundle branch-block pattern complexes (Fig. 5.8). Many modern pacemakers are programmable, and, on reducing the rate, the patient's own, slower, rhythm will be revealed for diagnostic analysis. Non-programmable systems can be inhibited as follows: an external pacing box is attached by electrodes applied to the skin on either side of the implanted pacemaker. When the energy of the external system is increased, the pacemaker will usually detect this and be inhibited. Clearly these procedures should only be performed in patients who are not totally dependent on their pacemaker, and should be performed with the patient on a cardiac monitor.

Normal pacing function can produce non-specific T-wave inversion which may not be ischaemic in origin, and this finding in the presence of recent pacing should not be overinterpreted.

Pre-excitation (Fig. 5.9)

In the Wolff—Parkinson—White (WPW) syndrome, the ECG may mimic the changes of infarction: the condition is characterized by a short PR interval and a slurred (delta) R wave. In the presence of this ECG change, no useful comment may be made concerning the possibility of myocardial ischaemia. The ECG change connotes an anomalous bypass tract between the atria and the ventricles, which may allow extremely fast conduction, promoting tachycardia.

Significance of changes on the admission ECG

The routine admission ECG contains much prognostic information: in the European Cooperative Study Group trial, patients with high ST elevation (sum of ST elevations at 60 ms after the the J point of 20 mm or more) had significantly greater enzymatic infarct size, and this was associated with a higher hospital mortality. There was also a higher mortality associated with reciprocal ST segment depression, and this was independent of the ST elevation (Willems *et al.* 1990). The evidence indicates that the greater the total ST segment shifts the greater is the myocardium in jeopardy, and the greater is the potential for salvage.

TRIAGE

Several triage decision aids have been described, some relating to decision-making at the time of the initial presentation in terms of the likelihood of acute myocardial ischaemia (Pozen *et al.* 1980, 1984; Goldman *et al.* 1982, 1988), others to specific complications of acute ischaemia (Mulley *et al.* 1980; Brush *et al.* 1985; Tierney *et al.* 1985).

Identifying the one-third of patients with true myocardial ischaemia (unstable angina or acute myocardial infarction) continues to be problematical. We still send home 5 per cent of patients with acute myocardial infarction through oversight, and admit, probably unnecessarily, up to 25 per cent of a coronary unit population who do not have acute ischaemia at all. Improving the efficiency of coronary care unit referral could have an important impact on the cost of acute coronary care: in the United States it has been calculated that up to four billion dollars are spent on CCU care for patients who prove not to have acute infarction (Fineberg *et al.* 1984). The ability of some investigators to achieve a reduction in CCU admissions by 30 per cent for patients without acute myocardial ischaemia indicates the potential for CCU triage (Pozen *et al*. 1984). These investigators have developed a hand-held, programmable calculator which computes a patient's probability of having acute cardiac ischaemia. The calculation takes only 20 seconds, and the probability is based on clinical features, including clinical presentation, history, physical findings, the ECG, sociodemographic characteristics, and risk factors. These authors reported no decrease in the admission of patients with acute ischaemia.

ANALGESIA

Analgesia should be administered promptly, since anxiety and pain increase myocardial oxygen demand, which is undesirable in this situation. Furthermore, the release of excess catecholamines may allow the development of threatening arrhythmias. Opiates exert favourable effects by being analgesic and anxiolytic, and they have desirable vasodilatory properties in addition, whereby they reduce pulmonary congestion.

- **Diamorphine** 2.5−5.0 mg should be used intravenously at 1 mg/minute in addition to increments of 2.5 mg at 10-minute intervals until pain is relieved.

The opiates may result in hypotension because of their vasodilatory effects, and they may also be associated with respiratory depression, especially in patients with airways disease, in whom a smaller dose should be administered in small increments. Any respiratory depression may be reversed with naloxone (0.8 mg intravenously); and this may need to be repeated at intervals of two minutes to a maximum 10 mg, remembering that the analgesic effects of the opiate will also be reversed.

- **Pentazocine** should be *avoided* as an analgesic in this situation, as it increases left ventricular pre- and afterload, which is undesirable.

- **Cyclizine** 50 mg should be used to limit the associated nausea of the opiate, and both should be given intravenously, to achieve a rapid and reliable response, but also to reduce the possibility of confounding enzyme release from skeletal muscle's interfering with the subsequent diagnosis.

- **Metoclopramide** 10 mg should be used in the presence of shock or left ventricular failure, to avoid the potential constrictor properties of cyclizine.

OTHER MANAGEMENT

A chest X-ray should be taken early after admission and again on discharge, but will need repeating during the admission if cardiac failure is present to assess its resolution. The performance of X-rays must not delay the administration of appropriate therapy such as thrombolysis.

A cannula should be inserted at an early opportunity to facilitate administration of therapeutic agents. This should be a sterile procedure, avoiding antecubital veins, which may be required for haemodynamic monitoring later.

Patients should be attached to a monitor and should be nursed if possible in a quiet room with the minimum of disturbance, providing them with as much reassurance as is appropriate.

Some units employ oxygen routinely; evidence suggests that it should be used in ill patients who are likely to be, or who are proven to be, hypoxic.

THROMBOLYSIS

Patients likely to have experienced an infarct should be considered for thrombolysis at the earliest opportunity after admission. The earlier the artery is recanalized the more likely is the benefit (GISSI Trial Study Group 1986). Every effort should be made to shorten the delay between presentation and administration of the thrombolytic agent.

Risks and benefits

The potential risks of thrombolytic therapy should be understood, so that an early decision can be made concerning the risk–benefit ratio of thrombolytic therapy. The GISSI study using streptokinase showed a 0.2 per cent (two per thousand) incidence of cerebral haemorrhage. The incidence of cerebral haemorrhage in the ISIS-2 study was 0.1 per cent (one per thousand), but there was no overall increase in strokes, as thrombotic strokes were fewer in thrombolysed patients (ISIS-2 Collaborative Group 1988).

Thrombolysis in addition to aspirin within 4 hours of infarction is associated with an up to 50 per cent reduction in the odds of death. ISIS-3 demonstrated that all three currently available agents were equally effective in terms of mortality reduction but that anistreplase and tPA were associated with a minor increase in cerebral haemorrhage (ISIS-3 1992). Following the publication of the European studies some concern was expressed, mostly in the USA, that tPA had not been properly tested, the short half-life of this agent requiring intravenous heparin. Furthermore, because tPA achieves earlier arterial patency, some held the view that tPA was the thrombolytic of choice notwithstanding the results of the European studies and the price differential. The GUSTO study (Global Utilization of Streptokinase and TPA for Occluded arteries) has addressed these issues: this study compared tPA given as a front-loaded dose over 90 minutes, with streptokinase and with the combination of the two with subcutaneous or intravenous heparin in the streptokinase group. Of 41 021 patients, those receiving tPA had an additional 1 per cent absolute reduction in 30 day mortality (6.3 per cent compared with 7.3 per cent in patients receiving streptokinase). The use of streptokinase and intravenous heparin and a combination of streptokinase and tPA did not improve significantly the mortality rate of streptokinase used with subcutaneous heparin. There was a 2 per thousand patient increase in cerebral haemorrhage associated with tPA (0.72 per cent) compared with streptokinase (0.52 per cent). However, patients aged more than 75 years had a 1 per cent increased risk of cerebral haemorrhage with tPA (2.08 per cent) compared with streptokinase and intravenous heparin (1.05 per cent).

In 2400 patients randomly selected for inclusion in an angiographic substudy, angiography was performed either early (at 90 minutes) or late (at 180 minutes, 24 hours, or 7 days). The 90 minute patency rate was 81 per cent for patients receiving tPA, 61 per cent for those receiving streptokinase and intravenous heparin, and 56 per cent in those who received streptokinase and subcutaneous heparin; at 180 minutes there was no difference in the patency for the respective thrombolytic regimes. The 30 day mortality was 9 per cent in those with occluded infarct-related arteries, 7.9 per cent in those with significantly impaired flow, and 4.3 per cent in those with widely patent arteries. The authors claim that these findings support the early opening strategy confirming a direct relationship between restoring blood flow early, salvaged myocardium, and survival (American Federation for Clinical Research, Washington, May 1993).

All of this translates into an absolute increase of 10 additional lives saved per thousand patients treated using tPA but increases the cost per life saved by four times. From the GUSTO study patients particularly likely to benefit additionally from tPA are those with anterior myocardial infarction, aged less than 75 years who present within 4 hours. To maximize benefit whilst containing costs it may be reasonable to target this population of infarct patients with tPA, employing streptokinase for other patients.

The EMERAS study did not show a significant benefit for patients treated after 6 hours but did show a trend in mortality benefit in those treated between 6 and 12 hours. However, the LATE study (Late Assessment of Thrombolytic Efficacy) has shown significant mortality benefit (odds reduction in mortality of 26 per cent) in patients treated between 6 and 12 hours with tPA (European Society of Cardiology, Barcelona, August 1992).

Currently, at least in Europe, the practice is to employ streptokinase in the hospital environment because of its clear cost advantage: anistreplase, however, has advantages in pre-hospital treatment, because of its easier administration. Following previous administration of streptokinase, tPA has the advantage of being non-immunogenic, and therefore will be unaffected by elevated antistreptokinase antibodies, which may render a repeat dose of streptokinase inert or give rise to hypersensitivity.

Finally we should be aware that the risk of thrombolysis is the same whenever it is administered: it is the benefit which decays with time.

Indications

Richard Peto from the ISIS group advises that on the basis of the available evidence we should be employing thrombolysis in patients presenting with symptoms suggestive of infarction who have accompanying ST elevation or bundle branch-block. We should withhold treatment from those with normal ECGs or those with ST depression, since the potential benefit in these patients, even if they are subsequently shown to have infarcted, is lower, and the unwanted effects of treatment may not be justified. Furthermore, age is not a contraindication to thrombolysis: the relative benefit of treatment is the same in the elderly, and, since their post-infarction risk is very high, the absolute benefit in the elderly is considerable.

Adjuvant heparin

There has been considerable discussion as to whether patients should receive heparin intravenously, subcutaneously (as in ISIS-3), or at all after thrombolysis. Particularly in the United States, where tPA is most commonly used, and where heparin is used intravenously, there has been the perception that heparin has been incorrectly employed in the European studies, and that tPA, with its very short half-life, has not been properly tested, and has therefore perhaps been unwarrantably disadvantaged. In ISIS-3 the patients who received heparin did have a slight reduction in mortality (5 per 1000 patients treated), but at the cost of an increase in cerebral haemorrhage (2 per 1000 patients treated). Additionally there were 3 more 'major' bleeds, but 3 less reinfarctions per thousand in heparin-treated patients compared to those receiving aspirin alone. Professor Sleight from the ISIS group has commented that a group of 4000 patients in ISIS-3 received non-trial heparin at their physicians' discretion either as high-dose heparin intravenously or subcutaneously: in these patients there was no difference in mortality between the thrombolytic groups, but twice the incidence of strokes. This must be interpreted with caution, as these are non-randomized data, but supports the possibility that intravenous heparin may not be required after thrombolysis.

Physicians' use of thrombolysis

In a survey of consultant physicians and cardiologists in 1987 and 1989 documenting the management policies for treating acute myocardial infarction, there was an impressive increase in the use of thrombolytic and antiplatelet therapies in this time-interval: the percentage of physicians prescribing antiplatelet therapy rose from 9 per cent in 1987 to 84 per cent in 1989. Similarly those using fibrinolytic therapy routinely rose from 2 per cent to 68 per cent. The use of other interventions for the management of acute myocardial infarction, such as nitrates, beta-blockade, and anticoagulants seemed to change little during this period, although the routine use of coronary arteriography and anticoagulants after thrombolysis fell substantially between 1987 and 1989, from 23 per cent to 4 per cent and from 24 per cent to 7 per cent respectively. The authors note that the acceptance of antiplatelet and thrombolytic therapy into routine management of acute myocardial infarction occurred during a time coincident with the publication of several positive controlled trial results. They suggest that the rapid acceptance of the trial results may have been due to the the consistency and reliability of the estimates of the size of the benefits of therapy seen in these unusually large studies (Collins and Julian 1992).

Who should and should not receive thrombolysis?

Patients within 6 hours of a likely infarct with ST elevation or bundle-branch block should be considered for thrombolysis irrespective of age. All patients should receive aspirin at the earliest possible time, and the initial dose should be 150 mg; evidence suggests that maximum inhibition of thromboxane B_2 may not occur for 24 hours with aspirin 75 mg (Reilly and Fitzgerald 1987). As an adjunct to thrombolysis, the use of heparin is associated with a small clinical benefit, but also with an increase in serious adverse events; but it is required when tPA is administered.

Currently my advice is to administer a thrombolytic within 6 hours of the patient's last pain, or later if the patient is still experiencing cardiac pain and therefore possibly still infarcting. We usually reserve thrombolysis for patients with ECG changes suggestive of infarction, in order to optimize the benefits of therapy and limit its adverse effects. Some flexibility should be applied, however, since it is difficult to establish the timing of the onset and end of infarction, and some benefit of doubt should be allowed to reduce the possibility of withholding potential benefit.

We should not give streptokinase, or anistreplase, to patients who have received this agent more than four days previously, in view of the evidence that antistreptokinase and neutralizing antibodies may be raised significantly from the fourth day until at least four and a half years after a previous dose—sufficient to neutralize the full therapeutic dose of streptokinase. Furthermore the presence of antistreptokinase antibodies exposes the patient to the possibility of hypersensitivity reactions (Lee *et al.* 1992a). This is an indication for the non-streptococcal derived tPA (tissue plasminogen activator).

In patients with a history of gastrointestinal pain or ulcer, prophylactic ranitidine 150 mg twice daily should be used.

The subclavian route must not be employed for invasive procedures in patients who have recently received thrombolysis or who are anticoagulated: it is not possible to press adequately on the puncture site.

It has been considered that thrombolysis is relatively contraindicated in patients who have had cardiopulmonary resuscitation, for fear of internal haemorrhage: Cross *et al.* (1991) have shown that, in 39 patients with cardiac arrest within 24 hours of receiving thrombolysis, no clinically significant bleeding complication occurred. The authors conclude that cardiopulmonary resuscitation is not a clear contra-indication to thrombolysis.

Contraindications

Thrombolytic therapy should be avoided in:

- patients who have undergone surgery within the previous ten days;
- patients who have experienced a bleeding ulcer within the previous three months or who have **active** peptic ulcer disease;
- patients with a systolic pressure over 200 mm Hg;
- patients who have undergone **traumatic** cardiopulmonary resuscitation;
- patients who have had a cerebral event or cerebrovascular surgery at any time;
- patients who have received thrombolysis with streptokinase or a streptokinase analogue more than four days previously (these should receive tPA (tissue plasminogen activator), because of the likely development of neutralizing antibodies);
- patients with a haemorrhagic diathesis;
- patients on anticoagulation; and
- patients who have recently had arterial puncture.

These are relative contraindications only, and the decision as to whether to proceed with thrombolysis should be made after consultation with senior colleagues in these more complex clinical situations.

Management of haemorrhagic complications

- Apply pressure where possible to site of bleeding.
- Any anticoagulation should be discontinued.
- If bleeding is severe give fresh frozen plasma and blood transfusion.
- Consider use of tranexamic acid to reverse the thrombolytic effect, in the dose of 1 gram by slow intravenous injection.

Cost-effectiveness of thrombolysis

The variability of cost-effectiveness resulting from different infarct sites, the size of infarction, the agent used, and the timing of administration has been investigated: Vermeer *et al.* (1988) have shown very much higher costs per life-year gained from inferior infarctions and from admissions more than two hours after the onset of infarction. Laffel *et al.* (1987) have demonstrated a more than 50 times increase in cost per additional survivor when thrombolysis is used after more than four hours on a small infarct than when used in under two hours on a large infarct.

Dosage of thrombolytic agents

- **Anistreplase:** 30 units intravenously over 3–5 minutes.
- **Streptokinase:** 1.5 megaunits intravenously over one hour.
- **tPA:** 100 mg (10 per cent by intravenous bolus, 50 per cent by infusion over one hour, and the remaining 40 per cent over the subsequent two hours. In patients who are less than 67 kg, the total dose should be 1.5 mg/kg.) Following the use of this agent heparin will be required, owing to the short half-life of tPA, which might predispose to early reocclusion in the absence of heparin.

Emergency angioplasty does not confer additional advantage over conservative management (TIMI Study Group 1989).

Unless there is a contraindication to its use, aspirin should be given at the time of diagnosis and then daily, and currently we are using 150 mg daily. If thrombolysis cannot be used, consideration should be given to giving aspirin at least, in view of the persuasive evidence of mortality reduction with its use alone in the ISIS-2 study.

REOCCLUSION

In a study of 733 patients in whom early patency of the infarct-related artery was achieved with thrombolysis, Ohman *et al.* (1990) reported reocclusion in 12.4 per cent on restudy before hospital discharge: only 58 per cent of these occlusions were symptomatic. Reocclusion was associated with twice the in-hospital mortality rate, more cardiac complications, and more deterioration of ventricular function compared with those who had preserved patency. The highest incidence of symptomatic reocclusion was within the first three days (first 24 hours in 50 per cent), and was associated with a high mortality of 26.7 per cent when patency could not be restored.

NURSE RESPONSIBILITIES

Patients should be as comfortable as possible, and if their condition is uncomplicated this may include resting in a chair if they are uncomfortable in bed. Certainly the elderly should be nursed in bed for only a minimum period, to limit the thrombotic complications of immobility, which are otherwise high in this group.

Patients should be offered a light diet, which initially at least should be a low-salt diet. Regular fruit and high fibre intake is useful in avoiding tiresome constipation, which might lead to undesirable straining.

For the first four hours after admission frequent observations are required (blood-pressure hourly and heart rate half-hourly), and these will need to be instituted again after any important and unfavourable clinical development. Thereafter four-hourly observations are usually adequate: after the first twenty-four hours a single daily observation of blood-pressure will usually suffice.

ECG monitoring

Reliably clear tracings are essential:

- Electrodes should be placed where they will not interfere with the positioning of defibrillator paddles or temporary pacing electrodes should they be required.
- They should be positioned where the skin is flat, and hair should be removed from the whole of the area needed for electrode positioning. The skin should be cleaned with alcohol to improve electrical contact.
- The unit needs to ensure that electrodes are placed in the same routine positions, so as to avoid having ECG changes which are due to positioning being overinterpreted as being clinically relevant.
- Patients will usually be monitored in the CR_1 (V_1) position, which allows P waves and right-bundle branch-block to be identified more clearly:
  —the negative electrode is placed below the right lateral aspect of the clavicle;
  —the indifferent electrode is placed below the left clavicle; and

—the positive electrode is positioned in the fourth intercostal space to the right of the sternum.

- The CR_6 position may be employed if an unsatisfactory tracing is obtained with the CR_1 electrode placing; placing the positive electrode in the 5th intercostal space and in the mid axillary line will increase the recorded voltages.

- Adequate ECG monitoring should be checked by nursing staff regularly, to reduce the possibility of missed events, but also to reduce the possibility of 'emergencies' that are due to ECG artefact. The gain control should be kept to the lowest position that provides an adequate trace, and the rate alarms should usually be set between 50 and 150.

Patient information

Patients should have their questions answered frankly and unemotively, and well-written literature (such as that from the British Heart Foundation) should be made available. There is an attraction in having all information concerning diagnosis and prognosis coming from one source, so as to avoid inconsistency and confusion.

REDUCTION OF INFARCT SIZE

Beta-blockers, by reducing heart rate and the force of left ventricular contractility, reduce myocardial oxygen consumption. Clearly this is desirable in acute ischaemia, as it may result in a reduction in the size of the area of myocardium at risk. These effects are particularly helpful in patients with high sympathetic activity following infarction. In early infarction atenolol intravenously has been shown to result in favourable improvement in mortality (ISIS-1 Collaborative Group 1988). Some centres employ beta-blockers as policy in this situation; these agents are of course avoided in cardiac failure or heart block.

Parenteral use of nitrates, by reducing preload, has beneficial effects in limiting infarct size, and again is standard therapy in some units. The dose of intravenous glyceryl trinitrate or isosorbide dinitrate is 25 micrograms/minute, increasing by 25 micrograms every 15 minutes until an optimal dose of 100 micrograms/minute is achieved. A systolic pressure of 90 mm Hg or less is a contraindication to starting this agent. An indication to reduce the infusion rate is a fall of more than 20 mm Hg in the systolic pressure or a sustained increase in heart rate.

The infusion may be discontinued after three hours, and a 20 mg tablet of isosorbide mononitrate may be administered.

ANTICOAGULATION

Some centres favour the routine use of anticoagulation in myocardial infarction in the absence of contraindications. Heparin in the dose of 20 000 units per 24 hours may provide prophylaxis. Its use remains controversial, but may reduce the incidence of mural thrombus and venous thrombosis, though this latter is a less frequent complication now that early mobilization is common after infarction. The role of anticoagulation is more established in patients with complicated infarction and low cardiac output, or those who are likely to mobilize slowly for any reason.

CARDIAC ENZYMES

Cardiac enzymes are helpful in either confirming or excluding myocardial infarction, and also provide a measure of the infarct size. Serial samples need to be taken to attempt to identify the peak enzyme release.

Venous blood samples should be taken regularly for estimation of AST, ALT, LDH, and, if it is available in your institution, CK. The first sample should be obtained soon after the patient presents, and a good opportunity to take it is when inserting a venous cannula, which is now common practice. Thereafter, samples should be sent to the laboratory at least daily for 72 hours. The sample should either be sent for immediate analysis or spun for later analysis, to prevent haemolysis's giving rise to spurious enzyme-release, making interpretation difficult.

None of these enzymes are exclusively released by cardiac muscle, and it is helpful to have more than one result of at least two different enzymes, so as to permit a more reliable diagnosis.

CK

CK begins to rise within 6 hours of infarction, peaking in 18−24 hours, and becoming normal after 72 hours. Elevated levels can also be seen in muscle disease, after extreme muscular exercise, and after intramuscular injection. A more specific enzyme for cardiac muscle damage is CK MB isoenzyme, but this is not widely available: a CK MB release of 15 per cent or more of the total CK is suggestive of myocardial infarction, and the estimation of CK MB release may be especially useful where patients have had intramuscular injections or cardioversion. This isoenzyme may also be elevated in circumstances unassociated with myocardial damage, as for example in patients with polymyositis, dermatomyositis, hypothermia, and muscular dystrophy.

The MM and MB isoenzymes of creatine kinase can now be subdivided into subforms which are released rapidly from infarcting myocardium in a characteristic time-course well before total creatine kinase increases. Assays for these subforms already exist as research tools, and they appear to allow the possibility of earlier confirmation or exclusion of acute myocardial infarction. Puleo *et al.* (1990) have reported that MB subform analysis reliably detected cardiac muscle necrosis in 59 per cent of patients with infarction within two to four hours of the onset of symptoms, and in 92 per cent of patients by four to six hours.

AST

AST (or SGOT) is elevated in about 12 hours, and peaks in 24–36 hours, becoming normal on the third to the fifth day. It is sensitive for myocardial infarction, but has poor specificity, since AST is widely found in other tissues, particularly the brain, skeletal muscle, and the liver.

LDH

LDH rises late after infarction, and can be useful in patients who present late. It peaks 24–48 hours after the onset of infarction, but can remain elevated for up to three weeks. LDH is found to be elevated even in minor haemolysis, and caution should be exercised in interpreting results if it is the only abnormality.

Myoglobin

Myoglobin is found exclusively in skeletal and cardiac muscle, and so it is elevated in patients who have received intramuscular injections and cardioversion. It is released early after the onset of infarction, with a peak between four and twelve hours. Lee *et al.* (1992c) have demonstrated that myocardial infarction can be excluded within four hours of onset using rapid analysis of myoglobin with newly available analysers placed in the coronary care unit. In this study a myoglobin threshold of 120 micrograms/litre at four hours gave a sensitivity of 88.6 per cent for diagnosing infarction in patients without ST elevation, a specificity of 99.8 per cent, and a predictive accuracy of 96.8 per cent. No patient with a myoglobin of less than 120 micrograms/litre at four hours was found subsequently to have infarcted. By way of comparison, a threshold for CK MB of 20 IU/litre at **six** hours was associated with a sensitivity of 81.6 per cent, a specificity of 92.3 per cent, and a predictive accuracy of 93.2 per cent. The authors have concluded that myocardial infarction can be excluded with a high degree of sensitivity and specificity within four hours of onset with myoglobin analysis, or within six hours with CK MB analysis. This would allow patients at low risk of events to be moved early from the coronary care unit, freeing beds for patients who may be more at risk.

Troponin T (TnT)

Troponin T is a structurally bound protein present in striated muscle cells, where it forms part of the troponin complex binding it to tropomyosin. Troponin T is present in both systemic and cardiac muscle, but the amino acid sequence in the two types of muscle differs, allowing antisera to be raised against cardiac-specific tropinin T. It has been shown to rise a median of four hours after the onset of infarction (range 1–10), and to be associated with a high sensitivity and specificity for diagnosing myocardial infarction (Mair *et al.* 1991).

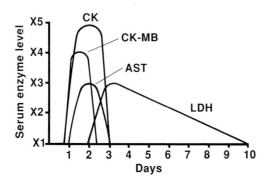

Fig. 5.10   Enzyme-release profiles.

Interestingly, thrombolysis causes an earlier release and peak of enzymes, owing to an earlier washout of released enzymes via recanalized vessels.

Generally a level of enzyme-release that is twice the upper limit of normal is considered significant, especially if there is fall into the normal range on serial testing.

RADIONUCLIDE IMAGING

While the cost and radioactivity hazard preclude the use of radionuclide imaging routinely, in many clinical situations this form of imaging provides valuable information. It is possible to use infarct-avid agents such as ^{99m}Tc stannous pyrophosphate for the diagnosis of myocardial infarction. The mechanism which allows this approach is the incorporation of the isotope into the hydroxyapatite that occurs with cell necrosis. Images become intensely positive one to three days after infarction, and usually return to normal by one week. It may be difficult, however, to differentiate between infarcted myocardium and overlying blood pool or bony uptake of isotope. Occasionally the scan pattern persists, and this is frequently associated with aneurysm formation. For pyrophosphate imaging, single-photon emission computed tomography (SPECT) appears to be superior.

Alternatively radiolabelled monoclonal Fab fragments of specific antibody to cardiac myosin can be employed. The mechanism is that rupture of the cell membrane resulting from infarction allows antibody to be attached to the myosin that has thus been exposed. In this form of imaging ^{111}In labelled antibody is injected and identified by planar or SPECT techniques: bony structures do not present a problem with this form of imaging, and scans tend to become positive soon after infarction.

Positron emission tomography (PET)

This form of imaging provides information on myocardial viability by detecting myocardial uptake of fluorodeoxyglucose (FDG), a glucose analogue. The FDG is taken up by living myocardium, but is not further metabolized. PET scanning identifies normal myocardium (preserved contractility and FDG uptake), irreversible tissue damage (no FDG uptake), and hibernating myocardium (uptake of FDG, but hypokinetic wall movement).

The role of this imaging modality is limited by its cost and the availability of facilities: the FDG, which has a short half life, has to be prepared for each study in a cyclotron.

Magnetic resonance imaging (MRI)

MRI scanning allows imaging in multiple contiguous planes, so that regional and global ventricular function may be assessed. This form of imaging produces tomographic images with excellent spatial resolution. Because of the three-dimensional nature of MRI, quantification of infarct size is possible using MRI-derived infarct volumes.

Certain elements such as hydrogen (abundantly available in the water of human tissues), when positioned in a magnetic field and excited by a pulse of radio waves, will emit a radio signal: collection of this signal by an appropriate receiver allows magnetic resonance studies to be performed.

Patients are placed in a strong uniform magnetic field, and a recording is made of the emitted signal following delivery of a pulse of radio waves. The detected signals are relayed to a computer, which reconstructs an image based on the amplitude of the emitted signal at each point over a slice through the patient.

When the radiofrequency pulse is switched off, the net magnetization vector gradually spirals back to its equilibrium position parallel to the applied field—this is called relaxation, and the rate at which it occurs is characterized by two time-constants T_1 and T_2. The relaxation times T_1 and T_2 are increased in myocardial infarction, and become apparent half an hour to three hours after coronary occlusion. Following established infarction, relaxation times remain high for several weeks.

Rapid imaging using the paramagnetic agent gadolinium allows assessment of myocardial perfusion and the recognition of myocardial infarction. The clinical use of this form of imaging is again limited at this time by availability, but also by the need for the patient to be inserted into the magnet away from ready clinical access, and usually in departments remote from the coronary care unit.

EARLY CCU DISCHARGE

The possibility of very early discharge (at day three) has been investigated by Topol *et al.* (1988). Patients with an uncomplicated infarction who had a negative thallium exercise scan were randomized to either discharge at day three or at days seven to ten. A total of 80 patients were randomized (the number eligible for early discharge on the above quoted criteria was not large). There was no difference in clinical outcome between the two groups, and in particular there were no deaths. The numbers returning to work were the same; but the group discharged early made an earlier return to work, and there was a reduction of one-third in the hospital cost associated with early discharge.

THE ELDERLY

Eighty per cent of the deaths from coronary heart disease in the United Kingdom occur in patients aged over 65 years. The elderly are often disadvantaged in terms of their share of resources, either because of ignorance of the evidence that therapy can have a major and favourable impact on their pathology, or because of 'ageism', whereby it is argued that finite resources should be reserved for younger patients.

Older patients are less likely to present with the severe chest discomfort which we classically associate with acute myocardial infarction. Indeed, many infarcts in the elderly are asymptomatic or 'silent'. The elderly are more likely to present with dyspnoea or confusion, and it has been suggested that this may relate to altered opioid sensitivity (Morley and Reese 1989).

Tofler *et al.* (1988) have reported on 631 patients aged under 65 years and 217 patients aged 65–75 years followed up for at least four years. At one year the mortality rate was 5 per cent and 19 per cent respectively for the young and old patients, and the four-year mortality rates were 13 per cent and 35 per cent respectively, both being a highly significant statistical difference.

The results of the large thrombolysis studies suggest that the relative benefit in terms of mortality salvage is the same for the elderly, and since their untreated risk is higher than for younger patients, the absolute benefit from thrombolytic therapy is considerable.

The risk of haemorrhage is greater in the elderly, and there is a large net mortality hazard in the first 24 hours after treatment; but, in view of the substantial total survival benefit, age should not be a contra-indication to thrombolytic therapy.

SUMMARY OF IN-HOSPITAL MANAGEMENT

1. Prompt establishment of diagnosis (history, examination, and 12-lead ECG).
2. Analgesia: diamorphine 2−5 mg IV with cyclizine 50 mg IV.
3. Oxygen if ill or in cardiac failure, or having proven hypoxaemia.
4. Insert IV cannula into peripheral vein and maintain patency with heparin flush. Take samples for cardiac enzymes, noting whether patients have received either intramuscular injection, external cardiac massage, or cardioversion, which would interfere with enzyme analysis.
5. Administer thrombolytic, if appropriate, at earliest opportunity.
6. Some units have a policy of routinely administering heparin to lessen the possibility of venous thrombosis and mural left ventricular thrombus. Our policy is to employ aspirin at the time of thrombolysis (the clot-lysing effect of the thrombolytic and the antiplatelet effect of aspirin are separate and additive (ISIS-2 Collaborative Group 1988)). Patients thought unsuitable for thrombolysis should be considered for aspirin alone. Patients receiving tPA should also receive heparin, in view of the short half life of this agent, the addition of heparin reducing the possibility of vessel reocclusion.

   All patients should be considered for intravenous nitrates unless they are significantly hypotensive.
7. Patients presenting with cardiac pain not thought to be due to infarction should receive beta-blockers, aspirin, and nitrates. Further pain may be an indication for intravenous nitrates: 1−10 mg/hour via an infusion pump according to benefit and blood-pressure effect. Pain despite optimal therapy, including the addition of a calcium-blocker, may indicate the need for cardiac catheterization to identify coronary disease, which may be threatening, and may require either angioplasty or coronary surgery.
8. Bed rest for 24−48 hours if uncomplicated, followed by slow mobilization. Passive leg movement should be encouraged whilst patients are in bed, to lessen the possibility of venous thrombosis. More gradual mobilization should be scheduled for patients with complicated infarction resulting in arrhythmias and/or cardiac failure.

9. Daily ECGs and cardiac enzymes should be requested for the first three days to increase the likelihood of a clear diagnosis.

10. Uncomplicated infarct patients can be discharged 5–10 days following infarction; they should receive clear advice concerning their activities, and much of this advice is presented in a satisfactory way in information leaflets available from The British Heart Foundation, 14 Fitzhardinge Street, London W1H 4DH.

6

Complications of myocardial infarction

CARDIAC ARREST

This can be usefully defined as sudden cessation of cardiovascular function. This is usually a legacy of cardiac arrhythmias. When it occurs early after infarction (primary ventricular fibrillation) it may not be associated with a poor prognosis provided successful resuscitation is performed. All personnel with patient-contact should be trained in efficient cardiac arrest procedures.

A cardiac arrest is a possible explanation when:

- a patient is found collapsed;
- a patient is in acute respiratory distress and cyanosed; or
- in the presence of a seizure.

Trained medical or paramedical assistance should be called at the earliest opportunity.

In patients with cardiac arrest:

- the pulse is absent;
- there is pallor or cyanosis;
- the patient is unconscious;
- spontaneous respiration may be present for many minutes, but may not be adequate for oxygenation; and
- dilatation of the pupils is usually a later, and therefore an unfavourable sign. It may be masked if the patient has received opiates. It is important to realize that some patients with dilated pupils make full recovery after resuscitation.

Cardiac arrest procedure

Patients should be placed supine on a firm, flat surface; this may require moving the patient to the floor. It is worth delivering a hard, firm blow to the sternum with the clenched fist. This has been demonstrated to return patients to sinus rhythm.

External cardiac massage is performed by applying cyclical pressure over the lower sternum: the heel of one hand is placed above the xiphisternum, with the other hand placed on top (see Fig. 4.1, p. 43). Pressure downwards should be sufficient to depress the sternum about 5 centimetres at a rate of about 80 per minute. Success can be assessed by the ability of an assistant to feel carotid or femoral pulsation and the maintenance of small pupils.

The most likely arrhythmia underlying cardiac arrest is ventricular fibrillation. Immediate defibrillation should be performed without waiting for an ECG diagnosis, as time is critical. Little harm results from inappropriate defibrillation, and the likelihood of success decays with the passage of time. Conduction jelly (in pad form if available) should be applied over the sternum and as far laterally as possible in an attempt to ensure that the current passes optimally across the heart (see Fig. 4.2, p. 44). The two applications of conduction gel must not be allowed in contact with each other, to prevent arcing of the current across the chest wall during defibrillation.

The initial two shocks should be 200 joules; if these are unsuccessful a 360 joule shock should be delivered, with external massage being continued between shocks to maintain a cardiac output.

Algorithm for the management of ventricular fibrillation

no pulse

↓

precordial thump

↓

cardiopulmonary resuscitation

↓

check rhythm

↓

if VF

↓

defibrillate 200 joules

↓

defibrillate 200 joules

↓

intubate (see **procedures**, Chapter 8)

↓

adrenaline 1:10 000 10 ml IV (or 20 ml endotracheal)
↓
defibrillate 360 joules
↓
lignocaine 100 mg IV (or 200 mg endotracheal)
↓
defibrillate 360 joules
↓
sodium bicarbonate 50 ml 8.4 per cent IV (**never** endotracheal)
↓
defibrillate 360 joules
↓
change to anteroposterior placing of paddles
↓
defibrillate 360 joules
↓
2 double (sequential) 360 joule shocks
↓
bretylium 400 mg IV
↓
defibrillate 360 joules
↓
2 double (sequential) 360 joule shocks

This algorithm presumes that ventricular fibrillation persists after each intervention.

If ventricular fibrillation does persist despite the above therapeutic measures other agents may be tried, as follows:

- procainamide IV 100 mg over 5 minutes, which may be repeated up to five times; or
- amiodarone IV 300 mg over 20 minutes.

The use of bretylium or amiodarone commits the resuscitation team to continuing CPR for at least 30 more minutes, because of the time-delay in the delivered effects of these two agents.

CPR should be performed between shocks and interventions, and this aspect should not be neglected for more than 10 seconds.

The pulse should be checked briefly after each shock, remembering that ECG monitors require a few seconds to recover after each shock.

It is vital to maintain a clear airway: the chin should be angled upwards, and the neck gently hyperextended, and dentures and any vomitus should be removed. The tongue must be prevented from prolapsing and causing airways obstruction, and an airway is useful in this regard. In the presence of inadequate respiration an endotracheal tube should be inserted. If ventilation is required, five compressions should be followed by a ventilation.

An early attempt should be made to gain reliable access to a peripheral vein for the administration of therapy. In view of the likelihood of venous collapse during cardiac arrest, the subclavian route may be quicker in experienced hands (see **procedures**, Chapter 8).

Patients found to be in asystole are significantly less likely to survive resuscitation, and defibrillation is unhelpful. An attempt to stimulate ventricular fibrillation should be made using pharmacological agents, so that cardioversion is then an option. Calcium chloride (10 ml of a 10 per cent solution), in addition to adrenaline (10 ml of 1:10 000) should be given intravenously. If unsuccessful these agents can also be administered by intracardiac injection, if the expertise is available. If this results in ventricular fibrillation, cardioversion should be performed as above. The coarser the fibrillation the greater the chance of success. If this results in ECG complexes which are slow or associated with a low output, isoprenaline should be employed, using 4 mg of isoprenaline in 500 ml of 5 per cent dextrose, and adjusting the rate according to response: remember that over-enthusiastic use of this chronotropic agent may result in the precipitation of serious arrhythmias.

If it is available, cardiac pacing should be considered for either asystole or profound bradycardia (see **procedures**, Chapter 8).

When to stop

If the outlook is considered hopeless, the most senior member of staff present should voice a quiet but firm decision to discontinue resuscitation.

It is likely that a few words of explanation, especially to the younger or more junior staff members, will be useful, and some of these may be overtly upset by the procedure and the decision to discontinue resuscitation.

It is always appropriate to express a few words of thanks and encouragement to the resuscitation team.

SUMMARY OF CARDIAC ARREST PROCEDURE

Make rapid assessment of patient's condition:

- is the patient conscious?
- is there a pulse?
- is there spontaneous breathing?

Summon help early rather than late.
Remember:

A—Airway.
B—Breathing.
C—Chest compression.

Give firm sternal thump.
Ensure the airway is clear and unobstructed. Use a Brook airway.

Fibrillation?

- Defibrillate as soon as the procedure is available, using 200 joules twice and then 360 joules if necessary.
- Establish intravenous access.
- If defibrillation is unsuccessful, perform chest compression and give intravenous lignocaine 100 mg.
- If unsuccessful, perform chest compression and give intravenous bretylium 400 mg.
- If unsuccessful, perform chest compression and give intravenous procainamide 100 mg.
- If unsuccessful, perform chest compression and give intravenous amiodarone 300 mg.
- If unsuccessful, the situation is grim, and a decision needs to be taken as to whether to continue with resuscitation.

Asystole?

Defibrillation is not effective; therefore attempt to precipitate fibrillation:

- Give intravenous adrenaline, 10 ml of 1 in 10 000; this can be repeated or given by intracardiac injection.
- Pacing should be considered if the facilities are available.

If the arrest procedure has continued for several minutes the patient's potassium and acid–base status should now be available, and may need correction; after several minutes of resuscitation it may be assumed that there is unfavourable acidosis, and 50 ml of bicarbonate 8.4 per cent should be administered intravenously.

If a slow bradycardia has been achieved give intravenous atropine 600–1200 micrograms.

An increase in rate and output can be achieved with intravenous isoprenaline 4 mg in 500 ml of 5 per cent dextrose and infused according to clinical response.

If at this stage there is no useful output consider discontinuing the resuscitation.

The BRESUS study has reported the outcomes of 3765 cardiopulmonary resuscitations in British hospitals: for every eight attempted resuscitations there were three immediate survivors, two at 24 hours, and one alive at one year after discharge. Survival at one year was 12.5 per cent including pre-hospital arrests, and 15 per cent when these cases were not included. In-hospital survival rates were best in those who arrested in the accident and emergency department, CCU, or other specialized unit. The outcome varied twelvefold in subgroups defined by age, type of arrest, and location of arrest. The authors conclude that 71 per cent of the one-year mortality in patients undergoing attempted resuscitation occurred during the initial event, and that hospital resuscitation is life-saving and cost-effective, and warrants appropriate attention, training, co-ordination, and equipment (Tunstall-Pedoe *et al.* 1992).

There is a clear need to canvas the opinions of as many interested parties as possible concerning the role of resuscitation in patients thought likely to develop cardiac arrest: any decision in this regard must be recorded and communicated clearly to the nursing staff. Aarons and Beeching (1991) have reported on the local use of 'do not resuscitate' orders in designating patients unsuitable for cardiopulmonary resuscitation in the event of cardiac arrest. Information was obtained on 297 patients who were inpatients in medical and surgical wards of a district general hospital: the prognosis had been discussed with 32 of 88 patients perceived by doctors as unsuitable for resuscitation. Of these 88 patients, 24 had orders not to resuscitate in their medical notes and only eight of these had similar orders in their nursing notes. The authors concluded that orders not to resuscitate are rarely included in the notes of patients for whom resuscitation is considered inappropriate. Elective decisions in this regard are not effectively communicated to nurses and there should be more discussion of patients' suitability for resuscitation between doctors, nurses, patients, and patients' relatives. Furthermore, suitability for resuscitation should be reviewed at every consultant ward round.

CARDIAC ARRHYTHMIAS

Cardiac arrhythmias are common early after infarction. Not all of these are threatening, and therefore they do not all require therapy. In general it is those arrhythmias which result in haemodynamic upset or which are of known prognostic impact which require therapy.

Tachycardia

- Regular tachycardia at rates greater than 130 per minute is unlikely to be due to sinus tachycardia, though this is not excluded.
- Regular tachycardia at 140−155 may be flutter with block.
- Regular rate at 160−220 may be supraventricular or ventricular tachycardia.
- Very rapid rates at 300 per minute or greater may indicate WPW pre-excitation with atrial fibrillation.

Sinus tachycardia

This is a heart rate of 100 or more beats per minute that is due to rapid sinus node discharge. It is less than 150 beats per minute unless the patient is exercising. Its onset and disappearance is usually gradual, and carotid sinus massage usually results in gradual rather than sudden slowing.

It is usually associated with anxiety, pain, cardiac failure, or an increase in metabolic rate, such as occurs in fever, anaemia, or thyrotoxicosis. Therapy should be directed at identifying and treating the cause, and antiarrhythmic therapy is not usually required.

Sinus bradycardia

This is associated with vagal stimulation, usually in the presence of inferior infarction. Treatment is recommended if it results in haemodynamic upset, in which case it usually responds to atropine 600 micrograms intravenously, and this can be repeated according to clinical response. Isoprenaline may occasionally be required. Haemodynamically important bradycardia not responsive to atropine may require pacing, which is described separately (see **procedures**, Chapter 8).

Supraventricular tachycardia

This arrhythmia (Fig. 6.1) is characterized by its rapid onset and termination, and by a rate of 150 per minute or more. It is usually narrow-complex, but confusion arises if the tachycardia results in rate-dependent bundle branch-block, and therefore broad-complex tachycardia.

The patient may be unaware of the arrhythmia, or it may produce cardiac pain, dyspnoea, or syncope. Most of these arrhythmias are re-entry in mechanism, and may respond to increase in vagal tone.

Treatment

• **Beta-blockers** are usually successful by slowing AV nodal conduction and increasing the refractory period, but should be avoided if ventricular function is significantly impaired.

Dosage: atenolol 2.5 mg IV at 1 mg/minute; may be repeated up to four times at intervals of 10 minutes.

• **Verapamil** is also useful as a result of its effects on both slow and fast AV nodal pathways, making it particularly useful in arrhythmias associated with pre-excitation, as in the WPW syndrome; but it should be avoided in atrial fibrillation or flutter complicating WPW pre-excitation: verapamil may promote anterograde conduction of extremely fast flutter or fibrillation down the bypass tract, leading potentially to ventricular fibrillation. Very rapid atrial fibrillation at rates of 200–250 per minute suggests underlying pre-excitation and a need to avoid verapamil. This agent should not be given intravenously to patients who have received intravenous beta-blockade.

Dosage: 5 mg IV over two minutes; may be repeated 5 minutes later if unsuccessful.

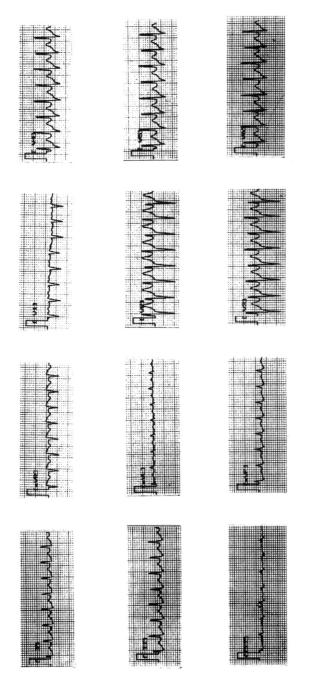

Fig. 6.1 Narrow-complex (supraventricular) tachycardia.

Verapamil should not be used in broad-complex tachycardia unless ventricular tachycardia can be confidently excluded.

● **Adenosine** is successful in aborting supraventricular arrhythmias conducting through the AV node.

It is also useful as a diagnostic tool, since while abolishing most supraventricular tachycardia it will not abort ventricular arrhythmias in general.

Dosage: 3 mg by rapid IV injection, followed by 6 mg after 2 minutes if unsuccessful and by 12 mg after a further 2 minutes if the arrhythmia does not revert to sinus rhythm. Patients should be cautioned about the adverse effects of flushing, dyspnoea, and choking, nausea, and light-headedness, which are transient. Adenosine should not be used in patients with airways disease.

● **Amiodarone**: refractory arrhythmias are likely to respond to amiodarone, but this therapy should be reserved for haemodynamically troublesome rhythm disturbances.

Dosage: 5 mg/kg in 100 ml of 5 per cent dextrose IV over 2–4 hours, followed by a maximum of 1200 mg over 24 hours. The arrhythmia may not abort immediately, and may take several hours to do so.

These rhythm disturbances also respond to appropriate pacing techniques: overdrive pacing or pacing at a rate faster than the tachycardia may allow capture of the ectopic focus, whereby gradual reduction of the pacing rate allows return of sinus rhythm. Underdrive pacing at slow rates can abort tachycardia by depolarization of one limb of the re-entry circuit, rendering it refractory.

Atrial fibrillation (Fig. 6.2)

This is a common rhythm in infarction (occurring in about 10–15 per cent of infarct patients), and is associated with an increased mortality, reflecting more extensive myocardial damage. Digoxin should be avoided, both because atrial fibrillation may be transient and well tolerated, but also because the inotropic effects of this drug are undesirable in acute ischaemia. In the absence of cardiac failure, beta-blockers are better employed for rate control in atrial fibrillation. Atrial fibrillation may give rise to haemodynamic disturbance because of the loss of the contribution of atrial transport to ventricular filling, in addition to which the fast irregular rate does not favour adequate ventricular filling.

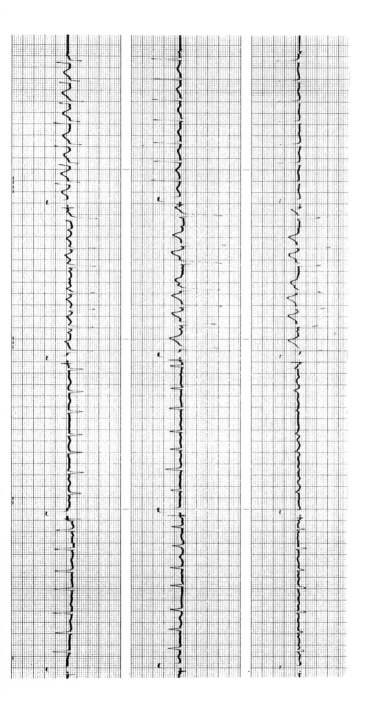

Fig. 6.2 Atrial fibrillation.

Management

If the arrhythmia is associated with important haemodynamic deterioration then cardioversion should be considered. Alternatively its rate may be controlled with either beta-blockers or verapamil. **(Do not use verapamil in the management of atrial fibrillation complicating the WPW syndrome—see supraventricular tachycardia, above).**

● **Digoxin**: if however digoxin is required (for example in the presence of cardiac failure), it can be administered orally or intravenously, the latter being reserved for those patients likely to benefit from rapid onset of action.

Dosage: oral: 1 mg in divided doses over 24 hours: 0.25 mg daily thereafter; but a reduced dose will be required often in the elderly or those with renal dysfunction.

Dosage: intravenous: 0.5 mg in 100 ml 5 per cent dextrose over 30 minutes. If indicated clinically this may be repeated over one hour.

● **Amiodarone**: intravenous amiodarone may convert the patient to sinus rhythm, or, failing this, control the rate of the atrial fibrillation, but should be reserved for those patients who are compromised by their atrial fibrillation. (Beward of digoxin toxicity in patients administered amiodarone who are on digoxin: amiodarone interferes with digoxin metabolism.)

Dosage: amiodarone IV 5 mg/kg over 2—4 hours and a maximum of 1200 mg over 24 hours.

Atrial flutter (Fig. 6.3)

In this arrhythmia there is rapid atrial depolarization at 200—300 per minute, with variable atrioventricular conduction. It is worth performing carotid sinus massage, which often results in either a higher degree of conduction block or return to sinus rhythm. Otherwise the management of this arrhythmia is similar to that of atrial fibrillation.

Heart block

First-degree block (PR interval longer than 0.22 seconds, (Fig. 6.4)), and Wenckebach (Mobitz type I second-degree heart block), where there is incremental increase in the PR interval with intermittent blocking of P wave conduction (Fig. 6.5), do not usually require treatment. Mobitz type II second-degree heart block (where there is a fixed PR interval with intermittent blocking of the P wave, (Fig. 6.6)),

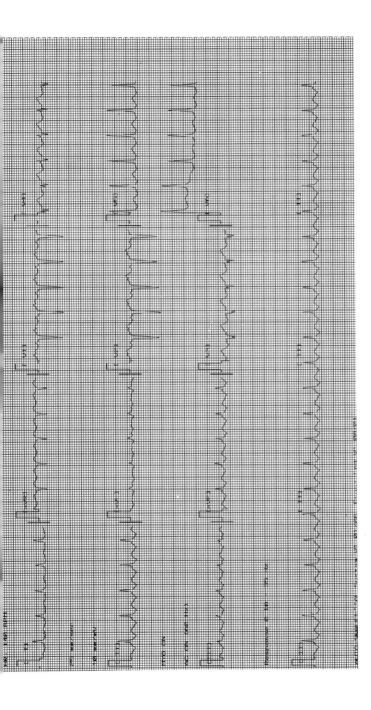

Fig. 6.3 Atrial flutter. Note the characteristic 'saw-tooth' pattern, which is well seen in the rhythm strip.

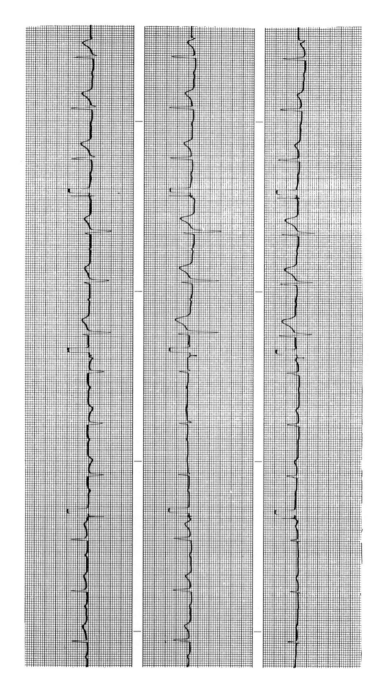

Fig. 6.4 First-degree heart block.

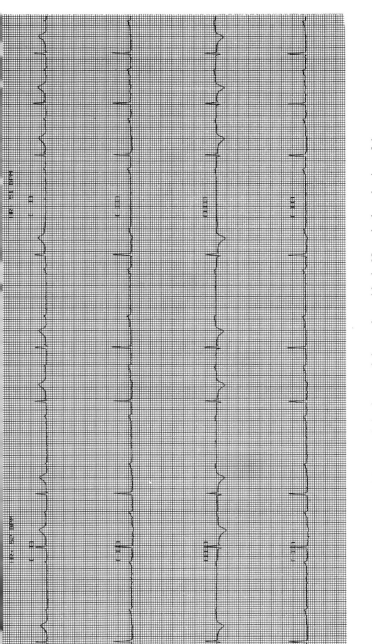

Fig. 6.5 Wenckebach second-degree heart block. Note the lengthening of the PR intervals until conduction fails and the cycle resumes.

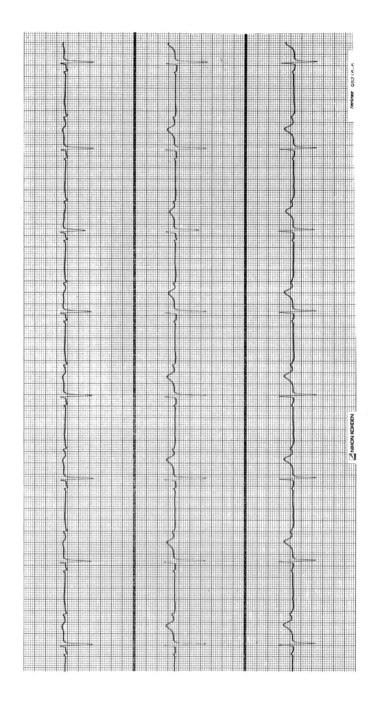

Fig. 6.6 Mobitz type II second-degree heart block.

should be treated with temporary pacing. These rhythm disturbances are usually relatively benign and often transient, and result from acute ischaemia of the AV node.

Complete AV block (Fig. 6.7) exists when there is no relationship between atrial (P wave) and ventricular (QRS) activity. Patients with anterior infarction and complete heart block usually have extensive cardiac damage associated with a poor prognosis (the mortality is of the order of 70–80 per cent). Despite the absence of persuasive evidence that pacing favourably affects mortality, this is considered an indication for pacing. In inferior infarction, complete block may be managed conservatively in the absence of haemodynamic disturbance. It is worth trying the effect of intravenous atropine 600–1200 micrograms, although the results are variable and unreliable. Haemodynamically unstable patients with complete heart block complicating inferior infarction require pacing. Therefore patients with anterior infarction and complete block should be considered for permanent pacing; those with inferior infarction should be observed for up to 3 weeks to see if sinus rhythm returns spontaneously before permanent pacing is initiated.

Patients with bifascicular block (right-bundle branch-block and left-axis deviation (Fig. 6.8) following infarction are considered for pacing in some units because of the increased likelihood of a higher degree of block developing. Left anterior hemiblock is the least unfavourable prognostically of the fascicular blocks, although still having a greater mortality than is found in those with uncomplicated infarction; it occurs in about 5 per cent of myocardial infarction. Left posterior hemiblock, occurring in about 1 per cent of infarction, and right-bundle branch-block, occurring in about 2 per cent, are associated with a markedly increased mortality, AV block being more common in these latter two conduction defects.

Ventricular tachycardia

Broad-complex tachycardia (Fig. 6.9), faster than 120 per minute and sustained for 10 or more beats, should be treated if it is likely to be ventricular in origin. Lignocaine is appropriate treatment. An IV bolus injection of 1–2 mg/kg should be followed with an infusion of 2–4 mg/minute for 12 hours.

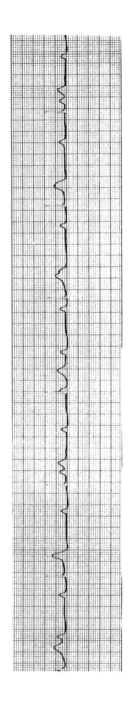

Fig. 6.7 Complete heart block.

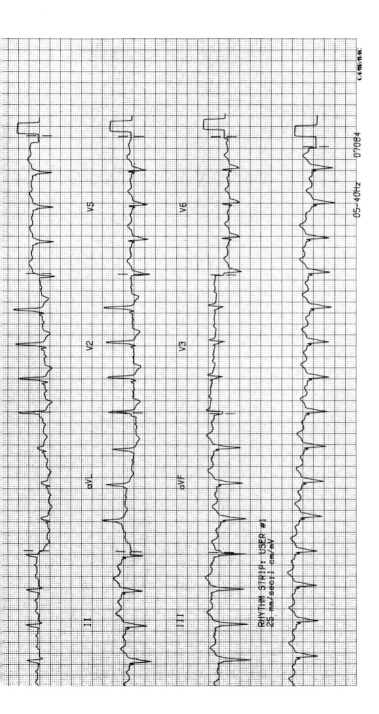

Fig. 6.8 Bifascicular block. Note the left axis deviation and right-bundle branch-block.

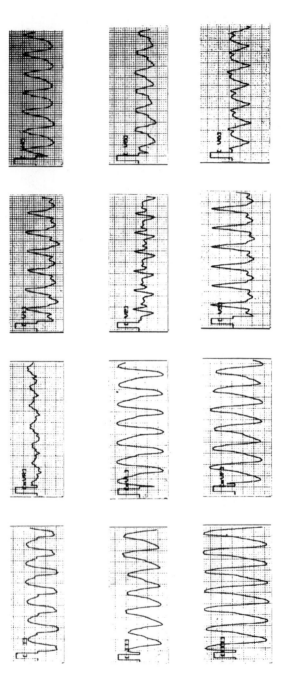

Fig. 6.9 Broad complex (ventricular) tachycardia.

Patients not responding may respond to:

- **Amiodarone**: 5 mg/kg IV over 20 minutes.
- **Procainamide**: 100 mg IV over five minutes, which can be repeated up to five times and followed by an infusion at 3 mg/minute.
- **Flecainide**: 2 mg/kg IV up to a maximum of 150 mg over thirty minutes twice daily. This agent is also successful in the management of re-entry arrhythmias and in arrhythmias associated with the WPW syndrome. **It should be avoided in patients with acute or recent myocardial ischaemia, because of the possibility of proarrhythmia, leading to an excess mortality (CAST Investigators 1986).**

If the arrhythmia is sustained and haemodynamically disturbing then cardioversion is the appropriate treatment, followed by lignocaine. Any hypokalaemia should be corrected, as it may be responsible for the arrhythmia.

If the underlying sinus rate is slow, this may be allowing re-entry arrhythmias, and atropine or pacing may abolish them.

If the tachycardia is associated with changing wavefronts (torsade de pointes) antiarrhythmic therapy may be inappropriate and pacing techniques may be required, and any potassium (and magnesium) deficit must be corrected. Clearly a senior or specialist opinion should be sought in these circumstances, and refractory arrhythmias may need overdrive pacing or more sophisticated electrophysiological techniques, such as programme stimulation.

How to differentiate supraventricular from ventricular tachycardia

When there is rate-dependent, bundle branch-block it becomes difficult to discriminate between supraventricular and ventricular arrhythmias.

The discrimination may indeed be impossible without some form of electrophysiological procedure. A bipolar pacing electrode in the right atrium can allow identification of atrial activity occurring before ventricular. However, there are some clinical clues:

The arrhythmia is more likely to be ventricular if:

- there is evidence of atrioventricular dissociation, seen either on the ECG, or as evidenced by irregular cannon waves in the jugular veins, or in the form of variation in the intensity of the first heart sound;

- there is QRS duration of more than 140 milliseconds, and an RSr pattern in lead V_1 and extreme axis shift favour ventricular arrhythmia;
- it is possible to identify ectopic beats in previous tracings which are identical to the complexes in the tachycardia, confirming that they are arising in the same chamber;
- there are capture beats where fortuitously a P wave has been conducted, giving rise to an apparently normal sinus beat;
- there are fusion beats where atrial and ventricular wavefronts collide, giving rise to complexes which have some of the characteristics of both beats;
- there is duration of more than 60 ms from the onset of the QRS to the nadir of the S wave in V_1 or V_2;
- there is a notch on the downstroke of the S wave in V_1 or V_2; or
- there is a Q wave in V_6.

There is more likely to be aberration of conduction if:

- carotid sinus massage abolishes the arrhythmia, as supraventricular arrhythmias may respond to this, unlike ventricular arrhythmias.

When in doubt—assume the arrhythmia is ventricular in origin.

Ventricular fibrillation (VF) (Fig. 6.10)

Four types of ventricular fibrillation are recognized:

- **Acute occlusional VF**: occurs within a few minutes of coronary artery occlusion, and is associated with most of the out-of-hospital deaths occurring suddenly after myocardial infarction.

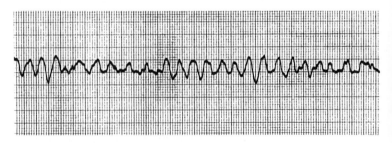

Fig. 6.10   Ventricular fibrillation.

- **Primary VF**: occurring within 12 hours of infarction, this form of VF is electrocardiographically identical to other VF. If reversed it appears to be associated with a relatively favourable prognosis. Lignocaine, magnesium, and beta-blockade prophylactically reduce the incidence of this arrhythmia.

- **Reperfusional VF**: the initial fears that this form of VF would limit the use of thrombolysis have been soothed by the recognition that although reperfusional arrhythmias are common, VF is unusual. Thrombolysis should certainly only be employed by those able and willing to provide resuscitation in the unlikely event of reperfusional VF. This form of VF may indicate a favourable prognosis if reversed, as it presumably reflects electrical reactivation of a significant amount of cardiac muscle following successful thrombolysis.

- **Late VF**: this form of VF probably reflects more extensive myocardial damage sustained during infarction, and is usually associated with an unfavourable prognosis.

There is persuasive evidence that VF cannot be predicted by monitoring for so-called 'warning arrhythmias'. The incidence of VF declines rapidly with time after infarction, and since VF prophylaxis is unreliable and potentially associated with serious adverse effects, it is usual practice (in the United Kingdom) to await the development of VF and to reverse it promptly.

Patients successfully resuscitated from primary ventricular fibrillation do not usually require antiarrhythmic therapy long-term, as the arrhythmia reflects acute myocardial ischaemia. It is common practice, however, to employ lignocaine after ventricular fibrillation, using a bolus followed by an infusion for 12 hours. Patients with secondary or late (usually days late) ventricular fibrillation require long-term antiarrhythmic prophylaxis with agents such as mexiletine, propafenone, or amiodarone (see **Cardiac drugs**, Chapter 9).

The risk of VF has been reported at 8 per cent in patients with an admission potassium of less than 3 mmol/litre, and 0.9 per cent in those with a level greater than 4 mmol/litre (Campbell *et al.* 1987). However, of the 25 patients with potassium levels below 3 mmol/litre, only two developed VF, the remainder having an uncomplicated course.

The procedure for the management of ventricular fibrillation is described under **cardiac arrest** in this chapter and under **cardioversion** in Chapter 8—Procedures.

Magnesium

All hypokalaemic patients who have threatening arrhythmias should receive magnesium in addition to potassium replacement.

Dosage: 8 mmol of magnesium sulphate over 15 minutes (via an infusion pump or diluted in 100 ml of 5 per cent dextrose) followed by 72 mmol over 24 hours (via an infusion pump or diluted in 1 litre of 5 per cent dextrose).

Ventricular ectopics

The concept of warning arrhythmias has been much questioned in recent years, and, generally, isolated ventricular ectopy is not treated. This is because none of the arrhythmias have been seen to have sufficient sensitivity or specificity in predicting subsequent serious rhythm disturbance. Certainly complex arrhythmias do precede ventricular fibrillation; but these occur with similar frequency in patients who do not develop it. Furthermore, a significant number of those developing ventricular fibrillation do not have warning arrhythmias. There is some evidence to support the anxiety that frequent R-on-T ectopics may precede ventricular fibrillation, and some centres consider this an indication for antiarrhythmic therapy with, for example, lignocaine. There is still no convincing evidence in support of employing prophylactic antiarrhythmic agents following infarction, and the policy of most units in the light of this is to await the onset of arrhythmias and to deal with them appropriately then.

Idioventricular rhythm (Fig. 6.11)

This is ventricular rhythm at rates less than 100 per minute, which is usually well tolerated and which usually requires no treatment.

Electromechanical dissociation

This arrhythmia is seen in cardiac rupture, sometimes temporarily after DC shock, and after massive pulmonary embolic events. There is electrical output, but no accompanying cardiac output. The likelihood is that the patient has cardiac rupture, however, and the outlook is grim. Adrenaline and calcium gluconate should be tried.

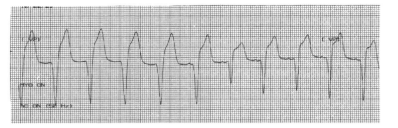

Fig. 6.11 Idioventricular rhythm. The presence of fusion complexes and capture beats identifies a ventricular rhythm.

CARDIAC FAILURE

Following myocardial infarction haemodynamic disturbance is common. It may result from left ventricular muscle damage, or it may be a legacy of hypovolaemia or due to the increased load resulting from acute mitral regurgitation or ventricular septal rupture. Most patients respond to conventional heart-failure treatment with diuretics, and thiazide diuretics are used for mild failure. For those patients with more severe failure, in whom a brisk and substantial diuresis is required, the loop diuretics are usually employed. They have an additional advantage in reducing ventricular preload, which is desirable in acute ischaemia.

- **Frusemide** is active orally and intravenously: 40 mg orally or intravenously, although a more reliable diuresis can be expected with intravenous therapy, because of the reduced bio-availability which may be present in cardiac failure.
- **Diamorphine** (2.5–5.0 mg by slow intravenous injection with an antiemetic) is helpful both for its effects on patient anxiety and because it lowers pulmonary pressure, which is desirable.

We should attempt to avoid the use of digoxin in view of its positive inotropic effects, which cause an increased myocardial consumption that is undesirable in this situation.

In inferior infarction, recording ECG leads $V_{3,4}R$ may indicate additional right ventricular infarction. In this situation, in spite of an elevated venous pressure, the cause of haemodynamic disturbance may be hypovolaemia, with diuresis leading to exacerbation of the problem: invasive monitoring allows for easier management of fluid requirements.

Invasive monitoring

In patients who do not respond favourably to appropriate therapy, invasive monitoring should be considered, using a flow-guided balloon flotation catheter. These catheters have an inflatable balloon at the distal end which allows them to be flow-directed to the desired chamber.

They are usually inserted under screening; but in experienced hands can be positioned by recognizing the appropriate pressure changes as the catheter enters the various cardiac chambers. They enable measurement of right-sided heart pressures, and measurement of mean pulmonary wedge pressure provides a close indicator of left atrial pressure, since, in the absence of significant lung disease, these are similar. The cardiac output can be derived if a thermodilution catheter is employed. The balloon catheter is inserted in a manner similar to that of the insertion of a temporary pacing electrode (see **procedures,** Chapter 8).

The information revealed by this procedure can alter the patient's management importantly: for example, if the wedge pressure (left atrial pressure) is low, then slow administration of fluid is likely to result in improvement, whereas administration of fluid in the presence of an elevated wedge pressure is likely to produce overt cardiac failure. Invasive monitoring can also allow the measurement of intracardiac oxygen saturations to detect acute intracardiac shunting, such as develops in septal rupture.

Furthermore, patients with elevated wedge pressures may benefit from vasodilation, such as that provided by nitrates, nitroprusside, salbutamol, or ACE inhibition (see **cardiac drugs,** Chapter 9). Benefit can be seen by improvement in intracardiac pressures, and in particular by reduction in wedge pressure; and the intention is to attempt to reduce wedge pressure to around 12 mm Hg.

The SAVE trial investigators (Pfeffer *et al.* 1992), have shown that in 2231 patients with an average follow-up of 42 months after myocardial infarction who have impaired contractility, (ejection fractions of <40 per cent), those randomized to captopril had a 19 per cent reduction in postinfarction mortality (confidence limits 3−32 per cent,

$p = 0.019$). There was a 21 per cent reduction in the risk of cardio-vascular death (confidence intervals 5–35 per cent, $p = 0.014$) and a 37 per cent reduction in severe heart failure (confidence intervals 20–50 per cent, $p = 0.001$). Recurrent myocardial infarction was reduced by 25 per cent (confidence intervals 5–40 per cent, $p = 0.015$).

It seems likely that ACE inhibition limits the threatening remodelling and infarct expansion that is known to occur after myocardial infarction.

Inotropic support

If the patient's cardiac output remains poor, inotropic support should be considered, bearing in mind the possible increase in myocardial oxygen demand, which is again undesirable. Dopamine in doses between 2 and 10 micrograms/kg/minute may usefully increase cardiac output with benefit. An additional bonus is dopamine's favourable effects on dopaminergic receptors in the kidney, preserving urine flow and renal function.

Indications for haemodynamic monitoring in myocardial infarction:

- to discriminate between low cardiac output due to hypovolaemia and cardiac failure;
- using oxygen saturation, to discriminate between traumatic mitral regurgitation and ventricular septal rupture;
- to allow more accurate assessment in patients treated with vaso-dilator or inotropic therapy; and
- to guide therapy in right ventricular infarction, where, although the venous pressure is clinically elevated, the appropriate therapy may be fluid administration and not diuresis.

CARDIAC PAIN

Sublingual GTN should be tried first, and may need to be continued intravenously if effective, in the dose of 1–10 mg/hour of GTN or isosorbide, according to benefit and effect on blood-pressure.

If this proves unhelpful then intravenous beta-blockade should be used in the dose of atenolol 5 mg over five minutes, repeated fifteen minutes later if uncomplicated. This should be followed by oral therapy in the dose of 50–100 mg daily.

If the pain is severe and unresolved by nitrates or beta-blockade, intravenous diamorphine 2.5–5.0 mg should be employed.

Consider the possibility that the patient is experiencing further infarction: if there is a likelihood of this, further thrombolysis may be indicated. If four days or more have elapsed since the last dose of thrombolytic, streptokinase or anistreplase should be avoided, in view of the likely elevation of antibodies, and in this situation tPA should be considered.

CARDIAC RUPTURE

One-quarter of all mortality in the coronary care unit may be due to cardiac rupture, and this is more likely to occur in the elderly, in women, and in the hypertensive.

The ISIS-1 study (of the effect of intravenous and oral beta-blockade on prognosis after myocardial infarction), showed a significant reduction in mortality in the atenolol group compared with the placebo-treated patients, but that that benefit was confined to the first one or two days after the onset of symptoms. A review of the records of the dead patients revealed that a large number of these patients died with electromechanical dissociation (continued electrical activity without mechanical function): nearly all the patients who had electromechanical dissociation and who underwent autopsy had experienced cardiac rupture, and significantly fewer had received atenolol: 17 in the control group and 5 in the atenolol group ($p = 0.01$). In 37 of the control group and 15 of the atenolol group electromechanical dissociation occurred, but autopsy was not performed (ISIS-1 Collaborative Group 1988). The benefit from beta-blockade early after infarction appears to be in preventing early cardiac rupture. The results of GISSI-1 and ISIS-2 suggest that thrombolytic therapy increases the risk of cardiac rupture on the first day, but decreases this risk subsequently. This had led some to suggest that early therapy for the management of acute myocardial infarction should be combined beta-blockade and streptokinase.

In the MILIS trial (Pohjola-Sinonen *et al.* 1989) cardiac rupture occurred in 1.7 per cent of patients. Patients with cardiac rupture had larger mean infarct size (peak CK−MB > 150 IU/litre), no history of angina or prior myocardial infarction, and signs of Q-wave or ST segment elevation on their presenting ECG. These variables identified a population in the MILIS trial which represented 22 per cent of the study group and had a ninefold increase in the risk of rupture. These findings support the suggestion that cardiac rupture occurs in patients who experience acute myocardial infarction as a result of sudden, total occlusion of a major coronary artery, and who have not experienced chronic myocardial ischaemia, which might have allowed them to develop protective collateral vessels.

Cardiac rupture should be suspected in patients who suddenly develop haemodynamic deterioration, and who may have a new murmur. Doppler echocardiography will assist in the differentiation between traumatic septal rupture and mitral regurgitation. The management of cardiac rupture is surgical; but many of these patients will not survive. Three factors have been identified as predictors of post-operative mortality: elevated right atrial pressure indicating right ventricular decompensation, systolic pressure of less than 90 mm Hg, and lengthy periods of bypass. Despite the risks, all patients with rupture should be considered for surgery, because the unoperated mortality is almost 100 per cent in this complication (Held *et al.* 1988).

CARDIAC TAMPONADE

In the setting of acute myocardial ischaemia, this is most likely to result from bleeding into the pericardial space and is associated with rapid and threatening haemodynamic deterioration.

Patients with tamponade will have tachycardia, elevated venous pressure, a small pulse pressure, and muffled cardiac sounds, and are likely to be hypotensive. They are also likely to manifest pulsus paradoxus.

Pulsus paradoxus

It is important to realize that this is an exaggeration of the normal phenomenon—a reduction of cardiac output with inspiration. It is detected by inflating a sphygmomanometer cuff to above the systolic pressure and during slow reduction of the cuff pressure noting the pressure at which the heart sounds can be first heard in expiration only, and then at what pressure they can be detected in both phases of respiration. The 'paradox' is the difference between these two pressures in mm Hg. The normal difference in the systolic pressure between the two phases of respiration is about 5 mm Hg: more than 10 mm Hg is considered pathological.

An alternative cause of pulsus paradoxus is obstructive airways disease—echocardiography will discriminate between these two.

CARDIOGENIC SHOCK

Myocardial infarction associated with extensive left ventricular damage may produce such significant impairment that cardiogenic shock results. This is defined as a condition where the systolic pressure is 80 mm Hg or less, with clinical evidence of reduced cardiac output: cold, sweaty extremities with oliguria. If invasive monitoring has been performed, there will be an elevated wedge pressure of over 20 mm Hg and a reduced cardiac output, with a measured cardiac index of <1.7 litres/minute/M^2. Patients with cardiogenic shock generally have 40 per cent or more of the myocardium damaged, and are likely to have proximal left coronary disease without collateral flow, to have multivessel disease, and to have experienced more than one infarction.

Goldberg *et al.* (1991) have reported that, in their study of more than four thousand patients, the incidence of cardiogenic shock remained relatively constant over a fourteen-year period at 7.5 per cent. The in-hospital mortality rate was between 74 per cent and 82 per cent over this period.

Ratshin *et al.* (1972) reported that patients with a combination of a stroke index below 2.3 litres/minute/M^2 and a left ventricular end-diastolic pressure greater than 15 mm Hg had a 100 per cent mortality.

Investigations

Cardiac ultrasound is helpful in this situation in being able to identify quickly and without hazard that the precipitating problem is left ventricular damage. Doppler is helpful here too in discriminating between the causes of cardiac murmurs, and in particular between acute mitral regurgitation and septal rupture.

These patients should have a urinary catheter inserted to enable accurate measurement of urinary output, as this is a valuable prognostic tool, as improving output is usually associated with improving prognosis.

The insertion of a Swan–Ganz catheter may have an impact on management since, as in the management of cardiac failure, patients found to be hypovolaemic (a low filling pressure or mean pulmonary wedge pressure) will benefit from fluid replacement: an attempt should be made to maintain the filling pressure at 16–18 mm Hg, which is the optimum to achieve the maximum stroke volume without precipitating pulmonary oedema.

Management

There is likely to be a need for inotropic agents, and left ventricular contractility can be enhanced by the use of dopamine or dobutamine: low-dose dopamine at 2–6 micrograms/kg/minute improves contractility, and has favourable effects on renal flow by the stimulation of renal dopaminergic receptors. At rates over 10 micrograms/kg/minute, increased alpha activity can give rise to an undesirable increase in vascular resistance.

Insertion of intra-aortic balloon counterpulsation (see **procedures**, Chapter 8) can result in impressive short-term improvement. This is usually reserved for patients who are being considered for cardiac surgery to repair a traumatized mitral valve or ventricular septum. It has not been shown to alter materially the prognosis in shocked patients who do not have reversible disease.

There is some evidence to suggest that emergency percutaneous transluminal coronary angioplasty (PTCA) improves the high mortality associated with cardiogenic shock, at least in those with anterior infarction and a left anterior descending stenosis (Lee *et al.* 1988).

DEPRESSION

Depression occurs in a significant minority of patients after myocardial infarction. Much can be done to avoid this by staff being optimistic, encouraging, and enthusiastic where this is appropriate. In addition, early mobilization and an early return to work provide reassurance to patients devastated by the possibility of becoming 'disabled'. Many will derive additional encouragement from performing a pre-discharge exercise test; and rehabilitation classes provide further reassurance in this regard. Pharmacology should be avoided if possible in the management of post-infarction depression.

DIABETES

Uncontrolled diabetes complicating infarction increases both morbidity and mortality (Gwilt *et al.* 1982). There appears to be a higher frequency of silent infarction in diabetics.

Patients found to have an elevated blood sugar (>10 mmol/l) following infarction should be managed with an insulin infusion; the blood sugar is usually easily maintained within the normal range with $1-2$ units per hour. Many of these patients will of course not require long-term insulin therapy.

HYPERKALAEMIA

A high potassium may result from an adverse response to potassium-sparing diuretic therapy, from over-enthusiastic replacement of potassium loss or from concomitant renal failure.

It may result in impaired intra-atrial and intraventricular conduction, and occasionally in ventricular fibrillation or even asystole. It may be accompanied by tall, peaked T waves and sine-wave-like ventricular tachycardia.

Threatening hyperkalaemia should be treated with an infusion of calcium: 20 ml of 10 per cent calcium gluconate infused over 5 minutes under ECG control. While acting to neutralize the effects of potassium on neuromuscular membranes, it has no effect on the potassium level, which should be managed with glucose and insulin and/or ion-exchange resin.

HYPOKALAEMIA

Hypokalaemia predisposes to arrhythmias, and is not infrequently seen in patients taking diuretics on presentation with myocardial infarction. It may be recognized on the ECG as a reduction in the amplitude of the

T wave, with increased prominence of the U wave, resulting in QU interval prolongation.

Repletion should be with oral therapy where possible: if the potassium level is greater than 2.5 mmol/litre and there are no arrhythmias, use oral KCl therapy.

If the potassium level is less than 2.5 mmol/litre, or there are arrhythmias, or following cardiac arrest, intravenous replacement should be used: 20 mmol KCl in 500 ml 5 per cent dextrose over 4−6 hours.

The use of a large vein avoids discomfort during infusion; but do not administer potassium into a line which may be lying in a cardiac chamber: this may precipitate arrhythmias.

Magnesium replacement should be considered for hypokalaemic patients, especially for those who had been on diuretics and those who experience serious rhythm disturbances (see **cardiac drugs**, Chapter 9).

MURMURS

The sudden development of a cardiac murmur or change in a previously heard murmur raises the possibility of the traumatic development of either a shunt at ventricular level or mitral regurgitation.

Ventricular septal defects

Rupture of the interventricular septum occurs in about 1−3 per cent of infarct patients. It occurs more frequently in the first week after infarction and in patients with their first infarction, who are less likely to have developed adequate collateral flow (Hutchins 1979). The development of septal rupture is often but not always associated with significant clinical deterioration, and there is a loud, pansystolic murmur at the left sternal edge.

Patients with traumatic ventricular shunts should be considered for emergency surgery: if their condition can be stabilized with medical therapy and intra-aortic balloon assist then angiography should be performed to establish the exact site of shunting and to examine the extent of coronary arterial disease.

Treated conservatively, 20–40 per cent of these patients will die in the first day, and 50–55 per cent will die within the first week (Vlodaver and Edwards 1977).

Four-year survival as good as 76 per cent has been reported in patients treated surgically for traumatic ventricular shunts (Daggett 1978).

Papillary muscle dysfunction

Ischaemia or infarction of the papillary muscle may give rise to disruption of the mitral valve apparatus. This may result in mitral regurgitation, which can be haemodynamically severe and even threatening.

Complete rupture of the papillary muscle results in severe mitral regurgitation, usually associated with acute left heart failure.

The murmur in acute mitral regurgitation is pansystolic, and is transmitted into the axilla, which helps to differentiate it from the murmur of a septal defect. If however the regurgitant jet is very eccentric, the murmur may be heard loudest up the left sternal edge.

Doppler echocardiography allows reliable discrimination between the two. Both conditions often respond well to vasodilation, which allows more forward flow and reduces the regurgitant volume, if the blood-pressure will allow the use of these agents. Most will also require the use of diuretics, in view of the frequently associated pulmonary oedema.

Early consideration should be given to the insertion of intra-aortic balloon assist, which by means of afterload reduction will also reduce regurgitant flow in favour of an increased cardiac output (see **procedures**, Chapter 8). This intervention may allow the the stabilization of the failing ventricle, so that surgery may be performed electively, rather than on an unwell, unstable patient, where the perioperative risks are necessarily increased.

PERICARDITIS

This may develop in the first few days after infarction. The pain is typically 'pleuritic', and a rub is heard in about 20 per cent of cases only. It is often associated with fever, a pericardial effusion may be present, and the ESR and white count may be elevated.

When it occurs late (3–12 weeks) after infarction it is called Dressler's syndrome. Some patients develop systemic symptoms, which include fever and malaise, in addition to the pericardial pain. The pain responds well to therapy with indomethacin 25–50 mg three times daily.

It is suggested that Dressler's syndrome may result from an auto-immune phenomenon triggered by products of myocardial damage (Fowler 1971).

PULMONARY EMBOLISM

Unexplained acute dyspnoea, often accompanied by low cardiac output, elevated venous pressure, and desaturation, may be due to acute massive pulmonary embolism. There may be coughing, haemoptysis, and marked pleuritic pain.

The diagnosis may be confirmed by a ventilation/perfusion scan non-invasively, or by pulmonary angiography where surgical removal of thrombus or thrombolysis is being considered. The ECG may show evidence of acute right heart strain, with an S wave in lead 1, a Q wave and an inverted T wave in lead 3 (the $S_1Q_3T_3$ pattern), and T-wave changes in the right ventricular leads (Fig. 6.12).

Most patients will be managed with anticoagulation and with heparin in the first instance, whilst warfarin is taking effect.

The incidence of this complication following myocardial infarction is greatly reduced now that patients are mobilized earlier.

REINFARCTION

Following acute myocardial infarction, reinfarction is associated with an increased mortality, often as a result of cardiogenic shock: Muller *et al.* (1988) have reported that those at particular risk of infarct extension include those with further cardiac pain following resolution of their infarct symptoms and those with non-Q wave infarction. In the double placebo cohort of the ISIS-2 study there was a 3 per cent incidence of clinically proven reinfarction during the period of inpatient stay. Following thrombolysis there may be an unstable endothelial lesion, perhaps with residual thrombus, and therefore the potential for a higher rate of reinfarction; and indeed this was increased to 4 per cent

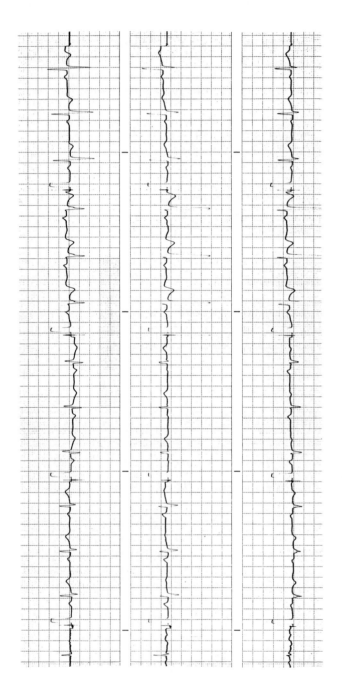

Fig. 6.12 ECG changes in pulmonary embolism. Note the $S_1Q_3T_3$ pattern. The ECG may be normal even in the presence of threatening pulmonary embolism.

in ISIS-2 (in patients receiving aspirin this rate was reduced to 2 per cent, still a significant population of patients who may require further thrombolysis).

In-hospital reocclusion of an infarct-related coronary artery in which patency has been achieved by thrombolysis has been reported to occur in 12.4 per cent of patients (Ohman *et al.* 1990). Only 58 per cent of these were symptomatic events; but reocclusion was associated with twice the in-hospital mortality rate (11 per cent vs 4.5 per cent), with more cardiac complications, and with more left ventricular dysfunction than occurred with those patients with sustained patency. Symptomatic occlusion occurred mostly during the first three days after infarction, and in 50 per cent in the first 24 hours, and was associated with a very high mortality, at 26.7 per cent, when the patency could not be restored. The authors concluded that strategies for preventing or managing reocclusion should be concentrated on the first three days after myocardial infarction.

Antistreptokinase antibody and neutralization titres may be elevated from four days to at least four and a half years after the administration of streptokinase: since this may lead to hypersensitivity reactions and the possibility of the therapeutic dose of readministered streptokinase's being rendered inert, non-immunogenic agents such as urokinase or tPA should be employed more than three days after previous administration (Lee *et al.* 1992*d*).

RIGHT VENTRICULAR INFARCTION

Patients with significant right ventricular infarction frequently have elevated venous pressure as a result of right heart failure, and a reduced cardiac output; pulmonary congestion is usually absent.

The ECG shows acute inferior or posterior wall infarction, and there is likely to be 1 mm or more of ST elevation in right-sided precordial leads (V_3R and V_4R).

Echocardiography or radionuclide angiography can also provide diagnostic information concerning right ventricular function non-invasively.

Despite the right heart failure, these patients often respond well to volume expansion, and this is an indication for balloon catheter monitoring (see **cardiac failure** above) to guide this therapy; and the temptation to give these patients large doses of diuretics should be resisted, as this is likely to compound the problem.

SHOULDER–HAND SYNDROME

This is now seen infrequently, and occurs weeks or months after myocardial infarction, especially if the patient has had prolonged immobility. The shoulder joint is limited, painful, and tender, and the hand may also be swollen and painful. It may have its origins in prolonged disuse of the arm at the time of infarction. Treatment is with physiotherapy and appropriate analgesia.

STROKE

Left ventricular mural thrombi occur in 20 per cent of patients with acute myocardial infarction not receiving antithrombotic therapy. This rate increases to 60 per cent of patients with large anterior wall infarction involving the ventricular apex, and associated with CK release greater than 2000 U/L (Fuster and Halperin 1989). The greatest risk is in the first ten days after infarction; but the tendency continues up to three months, and is related to the amount of damaged myocardium. This risk of cerebral embolism continues longer, however, in those patients with persistent ventricular dysfunction, atrial fibrillation, or cardiac failure.

Stroke resulting from cerebral embolism occurs in 1–3 per cent of all myocardial infarction, and in 10–20 per cent of those with large anteroapical infarction.

Cerebral embolism occurs in about 10 per cent of those patients with echo evidence of mural thrombus after myocardial infarction. In a prospective echo study to identify left ventricular thrombi after infarction, 541 patients were separated into two groups: 115 patients had definite evidence of ventricular thrombus, and 426 did not. Predictors of likelihood of embolization were: mobility of the echogenic mass, adjacent areas of hyperkinetic myocardium, and protrusion of the thrombus. Twenty-three per cent experienced embolic events prior to the first echo examination, and 7 per cent after the initial echo, supporting the suggestion that embolism is more likely to occur early after infarction. No cases of embolism arising in the heart were identified in those patients on anticoagulation (Jugdutt and Sivaram 1989).

Turpie *et al.* (1989) examined in a randomized trial 200 patients with acute anterior infarction who had not received thrombolysis: those patients receiving 12 500 units of subcutaneous heparin twice daily had significantly less mural thrombi (11 per cent) during the first ten days than those receiving 5000 units twice daily (32 per cent). Similarly the SCATI study (1989) showed an incidence of 17.7 per cent of mural thrombi in patients randomized to receive 12 500 units of heparin, compared with 36.5 per cent in the control group, and mortality was reduced from 9.9 per cent in untreated patients to 5.8 per cent in the heparinized group, both reductions reaching statistical significance: the short-term survival benefit was independent of initial thrombolytic therapy.

The likely impact of thrombolytic therapy on the formation of ventricular thrombi is uncertain, since this may have less to do with the fibrinolytic status of the patient than with residual left ventricular function.

7

Recovery

THE EARLY PHASE

It is recommended that patients should remain in bed for about the first 48 hours. Thereafter uncomplicated infarct patients are allowed to mobilize in a supervised and graded manner: on days 3–4 patients are allowed to sit out of bed and to walk a few steps around their beds. On days 5–6 slow walking around the ward can be allowed; and discharge can be from day 7.

Clearly mobilization will necessarily be slower in patients with complicated infarction, and their discharge will be delayed.

As early in recovery as is appropriate, patients should receive information about their condition either in the form of advice from health-care staff or from information booklets such as those produced by the British Heart Foundation.

A positive and reassuring attitude on the part of the staff is helpful, as many patients will be anxious and depressed at their situation.

Patients should receive advice concerning resumption of sexual activity and driving, and it is reasonable to suggest doing so at about one month after infarction. A return to work can be considered in uncomplicated patients at six weeks in non-manual occupations, but at eight to ten weeks for those who are in physically demanding jobs.

Patients may have particular anxieties concerning their livelihoods if, for example, they require a vocational (HGV or PSV) driving licence (see **vocational driving**, below).

RISK STRATIFICATION

Before discharge an attempt should be made to stratify the risk of the infarct patient. Patients who are elderly, those with continuing cardiac pain and failure, and those with complex arrhythmias are known to be at excess risk; but how shall we stratify the risk of those patients who appear to have made a good early recovery, but in whom we know there will be a significant early mortality in the first year?

Exercise testing

Many centres use treadmill exercise testing in this situation. Usually this is a limited exercise protocol equivalent to the order of exercise we would expect patients to be able to achieve prior to hospital discharge. In our hospital, patients aged 65 years or less who are able to perform exercise undergo a limited exercise test immediately before discharge; those who complete the protocol without symptoms or unfavourable clinical signs are considered at low risk, and are not exposed to additional investigation unless there is another clinical indication (Jennings *et al.* 1984). Those patients who have an abnormal test receive additional therapy in the form of beta-blockers if tolerated, and are considered for further investigation, which may include coronary angiography. Patients with an ominous development during exercise, such as those with exertional hypotension, an inappropriate heart rate of greater than 130 per minute, or deep (more than 2 mm) ST change at a low exercise level (Fig. 7.1), or those who develop threatening arrhythmias are usually observed in hospital for longer, and may need angiography before discharge, since some of them will not survive to their first outpatient visit.

Table 7.1 Early post-infarction exercise protocol

Minutes	Incline (constant 3 kph)
2	0%
2	3.5%
2	7%
2	10%
End-points:	—inability to continue;
	—2 mm ST depression;
	—BP fall > 10 mm Hg;
	—heart rate > 130/minute; or
	—sustained cardiac arrhythmia (not just ventricular ectopy).

Campbell *et al.* (1988) have reported a consecutive series of 559 hospital survivors of myocardial infarction aged less than 66 years in whom they designated 93 prospectively as low-risk: they were suitable for early submaximal exercise testing, and had none of the following risk factors: angina for at least one month prior to the infarction; symptomatic ventricular arrhythmias; recurrent ischaemic pain; car-

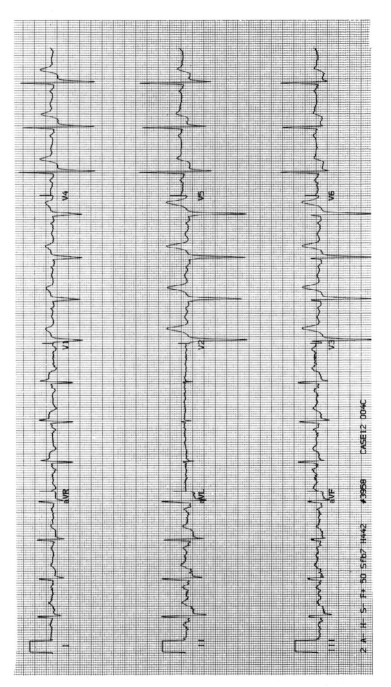

Fig. 7.1 ST depression in the inferolateral leads during a limited-protocol

diac failure; cardiomegaly; or an abnormal exercise test, manifesting either ST depression or poor blood-pressure response, or accompanied by angina. Altogether 301 patients were exercised, and their mortality over a median follow-up of 2.4 years was 10.2 per cent, versus 24.6 per cent in the 258 patients not exercised ($p = 0.0005$). Absence of clinical risk factors alone in the exercised patients identified 156 patients with a mortality of 5.4 per cent, versus 15.6 per cent in the 145 patients with at least one clinical risk factor ($p = 0.004$). The 93 patients prospectively designated at low risk had no deaths, compared with a mortality of 14.7 per cent in the remaining patients with at least one clinical risk factor ($p = 0.002$). The authors concluded that simple clinical and exercise test criteria can positively identify low-risk patients after infarction, in whom secondary prevention may be inappropriate.

Radionuclide testing

Exercise ^{201}Tl scintigraphy, however, provides increased sensitivity for detecting residual myocardial ischaemia, as well as information about left ventricular function (Varma and Gibson 1987). The frequency of detection of exercise-induced ischaemia is twice as high with scintigraphy as against conventional stress testing. Thus the error rate in falsely classifying patients at low risk is substantially smaller with scintigraphy than with stress electrocardiography, and it therefore provides more reliable risk stratification.

Arrhythmia detection

In general, serious arrhythmias occurring within the first few hours of myocardial infarction are related to the acute ischaemia: if the patient survives these events, the tendency for these rhythm disturbances is likely to diminish spontaneously with reversal of the acute ischaemia, and long-term antiarrhythmic therapy is unlikely to be required.

Late arrhythmias usually reflect the extent of myocardial damage, and there will be a need to investigate the possibility of improving ventricular function where this is amenable to manipulation. Some patients will require antiarrhythmic agents, and will need periods of dynamic ECG monitoring (Holter monitoring), to assess the degree of arrhythmia suppression (see **antiarrhythmic agents** in this chapter). Those patients who continue to manifest serious arrhythmias (sustained ventricular tachycardia or repeated ventricular fibrillation) despite antiarrhythmic therapy may require an electrophysiological study: this procedure involves placing electrodes into right, and usually also left, heart chambers to induce the arrhythmia by programmed stimulation, in an attempt to map the origins of the electrical focus, and to see if the arrhythmia can be generated after administration of antiarrhythmic therapy.

Resistant, threatening arrhythmias may be an indication for the use of an implantable cardioverter–defibrillator. By means of overdrive pacing, cardioversion, or defibrillation these devices are designed to treat drug-resistant ventricular fibrillation or tachycardia in the community. Fromer *et al.* (1992) have reported a series of 102 patients with haemodynamically significant ventricular tachyarrhythmias not suppressed by antiarrhythmic agents and treated with implantable devices. With a mean follow-up of 9.4 months (range 1−21) there was a 3.9 per cent perioperative mortality, and the actuarial 12-month survival rate was 91 per cent; 58 per cent received device therapy: 17 patients for ventricular fibrillation, 16 patients for ventricular tachycardia, and 28 patients for both. Using device memory data, 1235 spontaneous episodes of ventricular tachycardia were detected and treated in 43 patients; 1204 of these episodes received painless, initial antitachycardia pacing therapy, restoring sinus rhythm in 91 per cent. The 108 ongoing episodes received 209 multiple therapeutic attempts. Eighty-five additional overdrive pacing therapies restored sinus rhythm in 30 per cent. Initial ineffective pacing therapies received 51 cardioversion pulses. The success rate was 61 per cent. Some 286 spontaneous episodes of ventricular fibrillation were detected in 44 patients. Overall defibrillation efficacy was 97.6 per cent. In 9 per cent it was considered that inappropriate device therapy had been delivered: this is a potentially serious problem, whereby relatively benign, incorrectly identified supraventricular arrhythmias may be converted to more threatening ventricular rhythm disturbances as a result of the proarrhythmic effects of these interventions. The authors concluded that implantable cardioverter–defibrillators nearly eliminated sudden arrhythmic deaths in patients with documented, potentially fatal ventricular arrhythmias.

SECONDARY PREVENTION

Following myocardial infarction, secondary prevention attempts to limit the likelihood of recurrent infarction and sudden death. Although the risk is highest early after infarction, there remains a substantial threat thereafter. In the five years after infarction, 13 per cent of men and 40 per cent of women experience a second infarction (Kannel *et al.* 1986).

The greatest risk is associated with more extensive myocardial damage, and is therefore not amenable to manipulation, although the associated developments such as left ventricular failure and cardiac arrhythmias may be.

Smoking

In a long-term follow-up review, the mortality in patients who continued to smoke after infarction was 29 per cent at five years and 49 per cent at 7.5 years: those who discontinued smoking after infarction had a 14 per cent and 16 per cent mortality respectively (Aberg *et al.* 1983). The evidence is persuasive that patients should discontinue smoking after myocardial infarction.

Hypertension

Hypertension is an unfavourable risk variable after myocardial infarction. Generally it seems appropriate to manage hypertension after infarction similarly to its management in patients without infarction. Beta-blockade would appear to be attractive therapy because of its proven effects in secondary prevention. Those patients who cannot tolerate beta-blockade (particularly because of cardiac failure) are candidates for ACE inhibition, because of the favourable effects of these agents on ventricular function and remodelling.

Hyperlipidaemia

Studies of lipid-lowering have failed to demonstrate prognostic benefit following myocardial infarction. Notwithstanding this, and in view of the evidence that lipid-lowering slows progression of, and may even reverse, coronary arterial disease, it seems reasonable to measure cholesterol levels after infarction, and to consider lipid-lowering advice in those patients with unfavourable profiles (see **the cholesterol debate**, Chapter 2). These investigations should be delayed for about 12 weeks, since myocardial infarction renders cholesterol estimation unreliable: those with unfavourable lipid profiles should receive appropriate dietary advice, with only a minority requiring therapy, where their cholesterol levels are very high or there is familial hyperlipidaemia.

Stress

It has been suggested that so-called 'type A' personalities (characterized by hostility, competitive drive, time-urgency, impatience, and a sense of an effort-oriented person caught up in a joyless struggle) are more likely to develop coronary disease and to have a worse prognosis should they experience myocardial infarction. Patients able to change to a 'type B' personality were reported to have an improved prognosis (Friedman *et al.* 1982). However, other studies have produced conflicting results, and this concept therefore remains controversial.

Ruberman *et al.* (1984) have reported that two psychosocial factors impacted on subsequent mortality: the level of stress related to enforced retirement, marital separation, and financial problems; and, secondly, social isolation from family or friends. There was a doubling of mortality risk in those with high levels of stress; and there was an additive effect if both stress factors were present.

It does seem reasonable practice to advise patients with an unfavourable lifestyle or aggressive traits to moderate these where possible after infarction.

Beta-blockade

The role of beta-blockers in reducing the risk of death and non-fatal reinfarction has been established: 15 major randomized trials of beta-blockade have been reported, 12 of which have shown a lower mortality in the treated group compared with those receiving placebo. Combining the results of all these trials reveals a benefit of about a 22 per cent reduction in mortality and a 20 per cent reduction in non-fatal reinfarction. It seems that the reduction in mortality results from a reduced cardiovascular mortality, and an antiarrhythmic effect of the beta-blockade could be legitimately claimed in view of the demonstrated reduction in sudden death. These agents are of course anti-ischaemic, resulting in improved myocardial metabolism, and it may be that they are also associated with fewer plaque tears by limiting sudden undesirable increases in blood-pressure and cardiac contractility.

Aspirin

There is considerable evidence suggesting that platelets play an important role in atherogenesis, in thrombosis, and in myocardial infarction. Aspirin inhibits platelet cyclo-oxygenase irreversibly, and since platelets are unable to synthesize proteins the inhibition remains for the life of the platelet, about a week. These platelets therefore fail to produce thromboxane A_2, resulting in less platelet aggregation, and bleeding time approximately doubles for at least 24 hours. Thrombin, however, produces platelet aggregation independently of thromboxane A_2, and so normal aggregation occurs when thrombin-stimulation of platelets occurs. During anticoagulation, when thrombin is absent, aspirin can lead to severe bleeding problems.

Although the dose of aspirin required to inhibit platelet aggregation is very small, many physicians are employing the aspirin dosage closest to that used in the ISIS-2 study, 150 mg. It is likely that the aspirin is acting to prevent reocclusion of coronary arteries which have recanalized, either spontaneously or following thrombolysis.

In ISIS-2 aspirin was found to be very safe: there was no excess of major bleeds, there being just a 1 per cent excess of minor bleeding and bruising in those given combined streptokinase and aspirin. Aspirin was however associated with a 40 per cent reduction in stroke and a 49 per cent reduction in reinfarction, and was very well tolerated. These beneficial effects of aspirin were maintained for up to two years. From the results of the ISIS-2 study, for every 100 patients receiving aspirin acutely and then followed for two to three years there are four fewer deaths and four fewer major events such as stroke or reinfarction compared with what occurs with those not receiving aspirin.

Anticoagulants

Since reinfarction is likely to be associated with thrombosis, it seems reasonable to consider the use of anticoagulation after infarction. The evidence for the routine use of anticoagulation in the pre-thrombolytic era was equivocal, and is receiving renewed attention following thrombolysis in an attempt to maintain patency of the recanalized infarct-related artery. As has been discussed above, however, we now have persuasive evidence that aspirin maintains coronary arterial patency after thrombolysis, although where tPA is employed there will be a need for heparin in view of the very short half life of this agent.

There have been many trials of anticoagulation following myocardial infarction: many of these were performed in an era before the guidelines for good trial practice were recognized, and are difficult to interpret. Review of the adequate studies showed no significant reduction of overall mortality; but some studies did show favourable trends.

There has been much interest in the Sixty-Plus Reinfarction Trial (1980), in which patients over the age of 60 who had been on anticoagulant therapy for at least six months were randomized either to remain on therapy or to discontinue taking warfarin. In those patients randomized to remain on warfarin there was a substantially lower incidence of reinfarction compared with those who discontinued therapy, and there was a trend towards a reduced mortality in this group also. This was of course a study of the result of discontinuing therapy, which may not mean that patients who were on warfarin were benefiting from therapy—merely that they were disadvantaged, once on therapy, from the therapy's being discontinued. Notwithstanding this, patients who remain in atrial fibrillation, who have continued cardiac failure, or who have aneurysms of the left ventricle should be considered for anticoagulation, as their risk of systemic embolism is high: those in atrial fibrillation have a 5—8 per cent risk of stroke per year (a fivefold increase in risk); while those with dilated left ventricles have a 3.5 per cent risk of stroke per year, and this is doubled if the patient is in atrial fibrillation. This compares with a risk of 0.5 per cent of stroke in patients with 'lone' atrial fibrillation, unassociated with structural cardiac disease.

In considering patients for warfarin therapy, regard should be paid to the adverse effects of this treatment too: Edmunds (1982) has reported between 0 and 1.1 fatal events per 100 patient-years of warfarin therapy, with a weighted mean of 0.17 fatal complications per 100 patient-years. In addition, non-fatal complications occurred at a rate of 0.5—6.3 per 100 patient-years, with a weighted mean of 2.2 events.

Calcium antagonists

The available evidence suggests that, in general, these agents are not as successful as beta-blockade in secondary prevention after infarction. The SPRINT study (1988) using nifedipine failed to show benefit, although a study with diltiazem in non-Q wave infarction showed a reduction in reinfarction, but not in mortality (Gibson *et al.* 1986). This was a study involving relatively few patients, and the Multicentre Diltiazem Post-infarction Trial (1988) involving 3000 patients did not show overall mortality reduction in long-term follow-up. In this study those patients receiving diltiazem who had experienced cardiac failure had a higher mortality on diltiazem than those on placebo. However, those who had not experienced this complication had a significantly lower mortality on active therapy.

In the Danish Verapamil Infarction Trial-(DAVIT I 1984), where verapamil was started in the acute phase and continued for six months, no significant reductions in mortality and reinfarction rates were discovered. Subgroup analysis showed that there was a significant reduction in mortality between days 22 and 180 in patients treated with verapamil, suggesting that verapamil in the acute phase of infarction might be hazardous; this led to another trial of late intervention with verapamil, DAVIT II (1990). In this study verapamil was started in the second week after infarction and continued for up to eighteen months. Again there was no significant mortality reduction. However, in those patients without cardiac failure there was a significant mortality-reduction in patients randomized to receive verapamil: 7.7 per cent, compared with 11.8 per cent in the control group ($p=0.02$); in those with cardiac failure the mortality was slightly higher in patients receiving active therapy: 17.9 per cent and 17.5 per cent respectively (NS).

In summary, calcium antagonists should be avoided in patients with complicated myocardial infarction, and, although there may be a beneficial effect on the rate of non-fatal reinfarction, there is no evidence that they are better than beta-blockade for secondary prevention. There may be a role for these agents, therefore, in uncomplicated infarction in those patients unable to tolerate beta-blockade.

Antiarrhythmic agents

Sudden death occurs frequently after myocardial infarction, and it is tempting to treat patients experiencing post-infarction arrhythmias with antiarrhythmic agents. The results of controlled studies of these agents in the management of post-infarction arrhythmias have not been encouraging, however, and it is important to consider the proarrhythmic effects of these therapies. This anxiety is supported by the findings of the CAST study (1986), in which post-infarction patients whose ventricular ectopic beats were suppressed by flecainide or encainide were randomized to continue on the active therapy or to take placebo: there was a highly significant increase in deaths amongst those taking active therapy.

It is increasingly evident that, generally, complex arrhythmias after infarction are markers of more extensive ventricular damage, and it is this aspect which should be addressed, rather than treating the arrhythmias, which may be secondary.

There is a role, of course, for antiarrhythmic agents in patients with recurrent and threatening arrhythmias: these patients will require careful and expert assessment, which may require electrophysiological testing (see **arrhythmia detection** in this chapter).

FOLLOWING DISCHARGE

A gradual increase in daily activity is sensible, and further advice should be sought by the patient who experiences regular or limiting cardiac pain or troublesome dyspnoea.

REHABILITATION

Rehabilitation is a process whereby patients are restored to their optimal physical, medical, psychological, social, emotional, vocational, and economic status (Shanfield 1990).

In the United Kingdom rehabilitation has not been practised widely, because of the uncertainty as to whether it is associated with improved survival. There is inconsistency in the reporting of psychosocial benefit following cardiac rehabilitation: the randomized, controlled studies show less improvement in psychological well-being than the uncontrolled studies. It has been questioned whether the claimed benefit may relate more to close review of the patient than to participation in an exercise programme (Lipkin 1991). The conclusion of an extensive review of this subject was that special programmes of cardiac education, teaching, or psychological support and counselling over and above usual supportive care should not be recommended as routine measures after myocardial infarction (Greenland and Chu 1988).

It is the failure of several studies to demonstrate clearly a reduced mortality which has allowed the medical profession largely to ignore this form of therapy. This may relate to problems of study-design, with low-risk patients being recruited in addition to the number of recruited patients being small, resulting in a type II statistical error. However, this may have to be reviewed in the light of an overview of 22 studies of rehabilitation involving exercise (O'Connor *et al.* 1989). In this study there was a 20 per cent reduction in overall mortality throughout at least three years; this result is apparent one year after randomization, is statistically significant, and persists throughout follow-up. Furthermore, the confidence limits do not include unity, which implies that the likelihood that this result is due to chance is remote. It is likely therefore that previous studies had merely been too small to demonstrate benefits.

In summary, it is probably desirable for uncomplicated post-infarction patients to attend for rehabilitation in the early weeks after infarction. This programme should include the opportunity to address questions related to the return to activities such as driving, sex, and employment and to provide dietary advice where appropriate, and should include a graded treadmill-exercise component to improve cardiorespiratory fitness. Furthermore, it provides an opportunity to identify continuing cardiac problems and complications which might benefit from earlier intervention.

EMPLOYMENT

Studies suggest that about 50–70 per cent of patients return to work after myocardial infarction. Monpere *et al.* (1988) reported that 72.3 per cent of patients return to work at 12 months; but in only 13.4 per cent were medical factors responsible for failure to return. Social and psychological factors were responsible for the remainder of the non-return to previous employment. Fioretti *et al.* (1988) reported that white-collar workers were more likely to return to previous employment, with 68 per cent doing so, than blue-collar workers, at 52 per cent. Additional variables impacting on patients' ability to resume working were age, educational status, and psychological factors (Turkulin *et al.* 1988).

Vocational driving

The Driver and Vehicle Licensing Agency have recently proposed a change in their criteria for relicensing vocational drivers: a person should be advised not to apply for or hold a licence to drive a large goods or passenger-carrying vehicle in the following circumstances:

A. CORONARY ARTERY DISEASE

1. If the driver has suspected or proven angina pectoris whether or not treatment has been recommended and/or medication is being taken. When the identity of the chest pain is in doubt an exercise test should be carried out according to the standard Bruce teadmill protocol.
2. Within three months of:
   a. Myocardial infarction or unstable angina;
   b. Coronary artery bypass grafting;
   c. Coronary angioplasty.

Provided that the applicant can complete at least three stages of the standard Bruce treadmill protocol, or equivalent, off cardioactive treatment for 24 hours, without symptoms or signs of myocardial dysfunction, licensing or relicensing may be considered no sooner than three months following the index event in 2a, b, and c. Those with a locomotor disorder who cannot undertake a standard Bruce treadmill protocol or equivalent should notify the Driver and Vehicle Licensing Agency.

Coronary angiography is not required. If it has been undertaken, the Licensing authority will be recommended to refuse the application or revoke the license if it demonstrates:
   a. Impaired left ventricular function (an ejection fraction of less than 40 per cent).
   b. Significant occlusive disease in the left main coronary artery or the proximal part of the left anterior descending artery proximal to the origin of the first septal and diagonal branches, or if two or more major coronary arteries are significantly diseased.

B. DISEASE OF OTHER ARTERIES

If there is:

1. An aortic aneurysm, with a transverse diameter of 4 cm or more, either thoracic or abdominal, unless there has been satisfactory surgical repair;

2. Confirmed peripheral vascular disease with signs or symptoms of cardiac dysfunction;

3. Dissection of the aorta;

4. Aortic root dilatation (more than 5.0 cm) from whatever cause.

Provided that the applicant can fulfil the exercise requirements included in paragraph A, licensing or relicensing may be considered in (1) if there are no other disqualifying conditions.

Licence duration: requirement for periodic review

An applicant or driver who has been permitted to hold LGV or PCV entitlement with a history of coronary artery disease or other arterial disorder will normally be issued with an annual licence subject to satisfactory medical reports. The driver should be assessed by exercise testing at three yearly intervals and should remain free from other disqualifying conditions.

C. HYPERTENSION

If at the time of the examination for the licence or while the licence is held:

1. The casual, resting blood pressure exceeds 200/110 mm Hg;

2. With established hypertension, blood pressure readings are consistently 180/100 mm Hg or more;

3. Treatment induces side-effects likely to interfere with driving ability.

D. ARRHYTHMIAS

Where a driver has or has had the following disturbances of cardiac rhythm within the past three years: bradycardia due to atrioventricular block or sinus node disease, or a supraventricular (including atrial fibrillation or flutter), junctional, or ventricular tachyarrhythmia unless all of the following conditions are met:

a. The arrhythmia has not caused or is not likely to cause sudden impairment of cerebral function or distraction of attention during driving.

b. There is no significant echocardiographic abnormality.

c. The exercise test is satisfactorily completed as above without the development of any of the above arrhythmias. Antiarrhythmic medication, if permissible according to d (below) need not be discontinued before exercise is undertaken.

d. Drugs (other than beta-blockers, verapamil, and digoxin) are not required to prevent paroxysmal arrhythmia.

In cases where there has been a single episode of arrhythmia and there is good reason to believe that it will not recur, licensing may be permitted. Ventricular premature beats occurring singly or as couplets do not necessarily constitute a reason for refusing or revoking a licence unless any other disqualifying condition is present.

Where the driver has an antitachycardia device or automatic implantable cardiac defibrillator, licensing will not be permitted.

Provided the applicant is asymptomatic, that there is no other disqualifying condition and that regular follow-up in a pacemaker clinic is being undertaken, licensing or relicensing may be considered in those with permanent endocardial pacemakers.

E. ELECTROCARDIOGRAPHIC ABNORMALITY

Where the electrocardiogram shows pathological Q waves in three leads or more, or left-bundle branch-block. (A Q wave is defined as having a duration of 0.4 second or more and an amplitude of at least a third of the succeeding R wave).

Licensing normally will be permitted if there are no other disqualifying conditions, provided the exercise requirements in paragraph A are fulfilled. Pre-excitation may be ignored unless associated with arrhythmia.

F. VALVULAR HEART DISEASE

Where acquired heart valve disease is present, whether or not valve surgery has been performed, licensing will normally be permitted provided within the last five years there is no history of cerebral ischaemia, no history of embolism, no persistent or intermittent arrhythmia, and no significant persistent hypertrophy or dilation of the left ventricle. Regular review may be required.

G. CARDIOMYOPATHY

Licensing will not be permitted in:
1. Hypertrophic cardiomyopathy;
2. Dilated cardiomyopathy;
3. After heart or heart/lung transplantation.

H. CONGENITAL HEART DISORDER

More complex congenital heart disorders are likely to disqualify unless surgical repair has been undertaken and there is no arrhythmia or pulmonary hypertension. Permissible minor congenital heart disorders include mild pulmonary stenosis, atrial and small ventricular septal defects, bicuspid aortic valves and mild aortic stenosis, patent ductus arteriosus and aortic coarctation with a minor gradient and no systemic hypertension, and total anomalous pulmonary venous drainage provided there are no other disqualifying conditions.

Further information may be obtained from the Medical Adviser, Driver and Vehicle Licensing Centre, Medical Advisory Branch, Oldway centre, 36 Orchard Street, Swansea, SA1 1TU. Telephone: 0792 304747; Facsimile: 0792 304185.
These recommendations replace those published by The Medical Commission on Accident Prevention in 1985.

THE ROLE OF THE GENERAL PRACTITIONER

Following discharge from hospital, there will be a clear need for consistency in the management and advice which patients receive. It is to be hoped that, before discharge, a management plan will have been formulated in terms of discharge therapy, rate of return to previous activities where appropriate, and arrangements for further follow-up and investigation. While this should have been discussed with the patient in hospital, it is recognized that many patients will have little recall of this advice, and the helpful literature published by organizations such as The British Heart Foundation, and distributed by many departments of cardiology, will be helpful in this regard.

The responsibility of the general practitioner will be to reinforce the messages initially raised in hospital: among them will be both those relating to the modification of risk factors and those about the optimum timing of return to driving, sexual activity, and employment. It is essential that patients receive strong messages conerning the need for risk-factor change: without this emphasis patients are likely to interpret the need for risk-factor change as relatively unimportant. Clearly, spouses and other family members may be effective allies in urging upon patients the need for lifestyle change, and indeed in auditing these changes.

There is an important role for the general practitioner in identifying unfavourable developments after discharge: these will include post-infarction cardiac pain, cardiac failure, the development of loud murmurs which had not been recognized previously, and adverse effects of therapy. Many of these patients will require earlier referral back to the cardiac centre, since the occurrence of these cardiac complications after infarction may connote an unfavourable prognosis that may be reversible following appropriate investigation and treatment.

There will be a need to provide emotional support for the family of the infarct patient, who may also be traumatized psychologically by any myocardial event: they may require counselling on the implications for their own future. An unhurried, frank discussion of what has occurred and what may lie ahead, with reassurance where appropriate, may prevent anxiety and depression overwhelming both the patient and family.

Although it is desirable to recruit the assistance of the family in providing care and emotional support after myocardial infarction, this may result in increased anxiety if it is not handled delicately and sensitively: while it may, for example, be helpful to train family members in cardiopulmonary resuscitation, Dracup *et al.* (1986) have reported that family members taught resuscitation techniques were more anxious at three months than those not receiving instruction. No psychological benefit for the family member could be demonstrated, although it might have been expected that the provision of this training might have helped to lower the level of anxiety by allowing the family the perception that they could recognize serious events and deal with them.

FURTHER INVESTIGATION

Following myocardial infarction 10–15 per cent of patients who survive to leave hospital will die during the first year, and a large proportion of these will do so in the first few months after discharge. Those patients for whom an exercise test could not be arranged prior to discharge should have one arranged, so that the result can be available at the first outpatient visit, which should be at about six weeks. Patients with an abnormal response to exercise or those with cardiac pain or dyspnoea should be considered for further investigation by cardiac ultrasound or by MUGA scanning (imaging of cardiac function by labelling the blood pool with radioactive isotopes) if there is concern about ventricular function. Coronary angiography may need to be performed to establish the anatomy, and in particular to see the extent of non-infarct-zone coronary disease, in order both to help with risk stratification and also to help determine if coronary surgery is a management option.

Exercise testing early after infarction identifies a low-risk group without exercise-induced abnormality who have a one-year mortality of about 3 per cent; those with abnormal exercise tests (about 30 per cent) have a 19 per cent one-year mortality, with 80 per cent of the patients who die in the first year appearing in the group with an abnormal test.

It has been suggested that certain groups of patients with stable coronary disease have improved survival with coronary sugery: the most convincing evidence exists for those with left main coronary artery disease and those with severe three-vessel disease (Takaro *et al.* 1976; Chaitman *et al.* 1981; European Coronary Surgery Study Group 1980). Since up to 10 per cent of patients after infarction will have left main-stem disease, and about 30 per cent will have three-vessel disease, these findings are of relevance to patients who survive infarction: lesions which might be better managed with surgery being found in up to 40 per cent of such patients.

All of this suggests that we should consider all patients for coronary arteriography after myocardial infarction, since the procedure is relatively safe and the anatomical information thus provided would be valuable in the management of these patients. This is not recommended, however, both in view of the significant resource implications and also because we believe we can identify high- and low-risk groups of patients non-invasively: Cross *et al.* (1992) have demonstrated in a study of 200 consecutive post-infarction patients that a positive exercise test and/or the presence of angina after infarction identified all the patients with left main-stem disease and 25 of the 30 patients in their study with three-vessel disease: none of the five patients with three-vessel disease which would have been 'missed' by this approach were referred for surgery. Fifty had negative exercise testing and did not experience post-infarction angina: their one year follow-up was uncomplicated by death, reinfarction, or the need for revascularization. The authors conclude that the infarct patient with severe coronary disease may be reliably detected by a history of post-infarction angina or a positive exercise test. Thus approximately 75 per cent of post-infarction patients (those with a positive exercise test or post-infarction angina) should be considered for coronary arteriography in an attempt to identify threatening disease that might be amenable to revascularization; while those patients with a *negative* exercise test who do *not* experience post-infarction angina do *not* require coronary arteriography following myocardial infarction.

Routine coronary arteriography should be delayed where possible to allow resolution of the unstable aspects of the coronary lesion morphology: Davies *et al.* (1990) have reported that after thrombolysis for acute myocardial infarction, angiographic evidence of the unstable plaque and associated thrombus were seen more frequently early after therapy, and that these features had partially resolved when angiography was repeated 2–10 days later. Delaying routine arteriography therefore allows a proper assessment of the residual anatomy after spontaneous remodelling has occurred. Those found at arteriography to have left main-stem or proximal three-vessel disease are considered for revascularization.

In summary, patients with cardiac pain or ECG changes on exercise after myocardial infarction appear to be at excess risk in view of the fact that they have myocardium in jeopardy: it seems reasonable to consider these patients for further investigation in the light of evidence that revascularization in certain groups of patients may improve survival significantly.

It is our practice to treat patients with an abnormal exercise test with a beta-blocker if tolerated, in addition to the aspirin which is routine therapy; those patients who are experiencing cardiac symptoms receive appropriate therapy in addition.

8

Procedures

ARTERIAL BLOOD SAMPLING

This may be required in ill patients to assess oxygen saturation and acid—base status. As with all blood-gas sampling, the laboratory should be advised of the the imminent arrival of the sample **before** arterial puncture is performed, to ensure that the laboratory is ready to process the sample without delay. Ice should be provided for transport of the sample to the laboratory.

A syringe should be prepared with 500 units of heparin and the air bubbles should be expelled. The puncture must be performed as a sterile procedure.

This procedure is of course contraindicated if the patient has a bleeding diathesis or has recently received thrombolysis.

Radial artery technique

● The skin of the non-dominant wrist should be prepared using antiseptic to which the patient is not allergic.

● Local anaesthetic (1 per cent lignocaine) is injected, using an orange 25-gauge needle, superficially in the skin overlying where the pulse can be palpated easily.

● Whilst the artery is being palpated with the first and second fingers, introduce a green 21-gauge needle attached to a syringe and on suction, between the fingers but at an angle of 45 degrees.

● Withdraw the sample, expel any air bubbles, and apply a blind sealing cap to the syringe, dispatching the sample expeditiously to the laboratory.

● Pressure must be applied to the puncture site for at least five minutes.

● Recheck that haemostasis has been achieved.

Femoral artery technique

The femoral artery lies medial to the femoral nerve and lateral to the vein, and may be easily entered at the level of the inguinal ligament. The nerve must be avoided by careful palpation of the arterial pulse before puncture. Entering the vein may give rise to problems of sample interpretation, as the blood will, by definition, be desaturated.

The technique is as described above for radial artery puncture in other respects.

The colour of the sample is not a reliable indicator of whether the sample is arterial, and it is only the pulsatile nature of the flow into the syringe which is proof of arterial puncture.

ARTERIAL CANNULATION

In some ill patients there will be the need to monitor arterial pressure continuously or to have frequent blood-gas sampling. This will require the insertion of an arterial cannula.

- The procedure must be performed under sterile conditions, with the operator wearing mask, gown, and gloves. The non-dominant wrist should be cleaned with appropriate antiseptic to which the patient is not allergic.

- Identify the best puncture site by careful palpation of the arterial pulsation.

- Infiltrate the skin overlying the puncture site with lignocaine 1 per cent.

- Introduce a short 18-gauge cannula into the artery by aiming the needle obliquely up the arm: arterial entry is confirmed by return of arterial blood up the cannula. Once the artery has been confidently entered (it is possible for only the bevel of the introducing needle to enter the artery, leaving the accompanying cannula outside the artery), advance the cannula whilst withdrawing the needle.

- Compression of the artery proximal to the puncture site allows haemostasis whilst a three-way tap is attached to the cannula. The cannula and tap should now be flushed with heparinized saline.

- Secure the cannula to the skin with a suture; the site should be covered with a transparent, occlusive dressing. The cannula will most often then be attached to a pressure transducer via a fluid-filled connector, and will be automatically flushed with heparinized saline by this system; alternatively the cannula will need reflushing after each arterial sampling. Before obtaining a sample the first 2–3 ml of blood should be discarded, to avoid contamination of the sample with diluting heparin.

Cannulae should be removed as soon as there is no longer a pressing indication for their retention, and should not usually be left *in situ* for more than five days: they may be associated with significant morbidity, and should be inspected frequently.

CARDIOVERSION

● **Elective:** in patients with troublesome or haemodynamically important arrhythmias (atrial fibrillation, or supraventricular or ventricular tachycardia) cardioversion is often successful in returning patients to sinus rhythm.

Where possible patients should be starved and sedated. In atrial fibrillation, anticoagulation should be started before the procedure, at least with heparin if time does not allow the establishment of anticoagulant control with warfarin. Warfarin should be continued for 6 weeks following the procedure to minimize the incidence of systemic embolization.

If time allows, digoxin should be discontinued; but if the indication for cardioversion is good, the presence of digoxin need not delay cardioversion unless there is evidence of digoxin toxicity, when consideration should be given to prophylactic pacing before cardioversion. Personally, I have never seen any complication associated with cardioversion of patients on digoxin.

In conscious patients, a short-acting anaesthetic is always required, as cardioversion is painful.

A defibrillator with a synchronized facility should be used: this will only allow energy-discharge on to the R wave, preventing the possibility of depolarization on to the T wave and the potential for ventricular fibrillation.

In atrial flutter, which may be very sensitive to low-energy shocks, an energy level of 25 joules should be selected initially. Levels of 360 joules may successfully convert patients with other arrhythmias that are refractory to lower energy levels, and there is evidence that cardioversion does not result in important myocardial damage (Metcalfe *et al.* 1988).

● **Emergency:** if the patient has fast tachycardia resulting in compromised haemodynamics or ventricular fibrillation, immediate cardioversion is indicated.

If the patient is unconscious an anaesthetic is not required, and a 200 joule shock should be employed and repeated if required, moving rapidly to 360 joules if unsuccessful (see **cardiac arrest procedure**, Chapter 6).

Factors which affect the success of defibrillation

● **Time:** the longer the period from the onset of fibrillation to defibrillation, the lower the potential for success. Prompt cardiopulmonary resuscitation will improve the likelihood of success by extending the interval in which successful defibrillation is possible. The value of trained paramedical and nursing staff in this regard is considerable: the ability for a trained coronary care nurse, alert and located near an arresting patient, to perform rapid cardioversion renders obsolete the practice of leaving the patient at rapidly increasing hazard whilst a doctor is summoned from a remote part of the hospital or from his bed.

● **Paddle position:** defibrillator paddles should be placed so that the heart is included in the path of the current. Two positions are favoured. In the anterolateral one paddle is placed on the upper right chest to the right of the sternum and below the clavicle, and the other paddle is placed on the lower left chest over the cardiac apex to the left of the nipple in the midaxillary line (Fig. 4.2, p. 44). The anteroposterior position involves placing the anterior paddle over the cardiac apex just to the left of the left sternal border, while the posterior paddle is positioned on the patient's left posterior chest beneath the scapula and lateral to the spine.

● **Energy:** in the emergency situation 200 joules should be selected. If the first shock is unsuccessful, the second should be at 200 joules, with subsequent shocks at 360 joules. In elective cardioversion, atrial flutter is often readily converted with low-energy shocks.

● **Impedance:** transthoracic impedance is the resistance to the current flow through the body, and is affected by paddle size, the quality of contact between paddle and skin, and the phase of ventilation (air is a poor conductor of electricity). The likelihood of successful defibrillation is increased: by employing appropriate defibrillation (or ECG) gel or impregnated pads if they are available (not all gel is sufficiently conductive); by pressing the paddles firmly on to the chest; by delivering the shock at the end of expiration; and, in persistent ventricular fibrillation, since repeat defibrillation reduces impedance, by delivering serial shocks without removing the paddles from the chest.

Defibrillation and pacing

Modern pacemakers have sophisticated filters to minimize pacemaker malfunction or reprogramming during defibrillation. Despite this, pacemaker disturbances may still occur, giving rise to loss of generator output, increased threshold with loss of capture, reprogramming to another function, and improper sensing. In an attempt to avoid this the defibrillator paddles should be placed as far away as possible from the generator. For example, placing the paddles in the anteroposterior position delivers the energy perpendicular to the sensing vector of the pacemaker, thereby reducing the potential for pacemaker damage. It is not necessary to adjust the defibrillation energy level, other than, as always, to use the lowest level which is clinically indicated.

Following attempted cardioversion, the normal functioning of the pacing generator should be established.

If a temporary electrode is in position it should be disconnected from the external generator, if this is possible in a patient who is not pacing-dependent.

Algorithm for the management of ventricular fibrillation

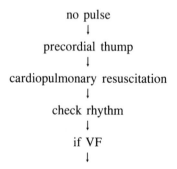

no pulse
↓
precordial thump
↓
cardiopulmonary resuscitation
↓
check rhythm
↓
if VF
↓

defibrillate 200 joules

↓

defibrillate 200 joules

↓

intubate (see **procedures**, this chapter)

↓

adrenaline 1:10 000 10 ml IV (or 20 ml endotracheal)

↓

defibrillate 360 joules

↓

lignocaine 100 mg IV (or 200 mg endotracheal)

↓

defibrillate 360 joules

↓

sodium bicarbonate 50 ml 8.4 per cent IV (**never** endotracheal)

↓

defibrillate 360 joules

↓

change to anteroposterior placing of paddles

↓

defibrillate 360 joules

↓

2 double (sequential) 360 joule shocks

↓

bretylium 400 mg IV

↓

defibrillate 360 joules

↓

2 double (sequential) 360 joule shocks

This algorithm presumes that ventricular fibrillation persists after each intervention.

If ventricular fibrillation does persist despite the above therapeutic measures other agents may be tried, as follows:

- procainamide IV 100 mg over 5 minutes, which may be repeated up to five times; or
- amiodarone IV 300 mg over 20 minutes.

The use of either bretylium or amiodarone commits the resuscitation team to continuing CPR for at least 30 more minutes, because of the time-delay in the delivered effects of these two agents.

CPR should be performed between shocks and interventions, and this aspect should not be neglected for more than 10 seconds.

The pulse should be checked briefly after each shock, remembering that ECG monitors require a few seconds to recover after each shock.

CENTRAL VENOUS PRESSURE MEASUREMENT

This may be desirable in unwell patients with cardiac failure, where there is uncertainty concerning circulating volume. It is important to realize that it provides little evidence of **left**-heart events.

● The venous catheter is inserted as described under **femoral vein cannulation** and **subclavian vein cannulation** in this chapter.

● Radiological screening confirms that the catheter is in a central vein.

● A three-way tap is used to connect the catheter to a CVP manometer and infusion set.

● Turning the tap allows the manometer to be filled from the infusion set; the tap is now turned to connect the patient to the manometer, and the fluid level in the manometer should be seen to rise and fall with respiration.

● A reference zero should be selected—either the mid-axillary point (needs to be marked for consistency) or the manubriosternal junction; and a spirit level should be used to line up this reference point with the manometer fluid level. This zeroing will need to be repeated every time a reading is obtained, unless it is certain the patient has not moved.

● The CVP is the level of the fluid in centimetres compared with the zero reference level. Following each measurement the tap should be directed so that there is slow flow from the infusion set to the patient, to maintain patency of the cannula.

INTRA-AORTIC BALLOON ASSISTANCE

In patients whose cardiac output cannot be maintained by medical treatment, mechanical circulatory assistance may be life-saving. Intra-aortic balloon assistance supports the failing myocardium by reducing afterload: a helium-filled balloon in the descending aorta (just below the aortic arch) is automatically inflated in diastole and rapidly deflated at the onset of systole. This is achieved by gating the inflation either to the dicrotic notch of the arterial pressure or the latter half of the T wave of the ECG. Balloon inflation displaces about 40 ml of blood towards the closed aortic valve, thereby increasing coronary arterial flow, which occurs predominantly in diastole and supports diastolic and mean aortic pressure. Deflation of the balloon immediately before systole creates a 'space' into which the left ventricle can eject with less mechanical effort because of the reduced resistance, and as a result myocardial oxygen requirements are reduced. Optimal balloon assistance may increase cardiac output by 50 per cent, and mean arterial pressure by 10–15 mm Hg (Dunkman *et al.* 1972).

Indications for intra-aortic balloon assistance

- Patients with acute myocardial infarction complicated by potentially reversible mitral regurgitation or ventricular septal defects;
- patients with severe refractory angina despite optimal medical therapy, requiring stabilization before angiography and possible surgery; and
- patients with temporarily stunned left ventricles who cannot be weaned off cardiopulmonary bypass.

Contraindications to intra-aortic balloon assistance

- Aortic dissection;
- aortic regurgitation;
- peripheral vascular disease; and
- circulatory collapse for which there is no likelihood of spontaneous or surgical relief.

Insertion technique

Although the balloon catheter may be inserted under direct vision by exposing the femoral artery, it is now more usually inserted by the percutaneous Seldinger technique, and clearly this procedure should only be performed by operators who are experienced in this technique. Detailed instructions are provided by the manufacturers, and the operator must be familiar with these before attempting balloon insertion. A description of the insertion technique is provided here for information purposes.

- Do not remove the balloon from the tray until ready for insertion.
- Under sterile conditions a Seldinger needle is inserted into the femoral artery in the right groin as during conventional angiography. Removal of the stylet allows insertion of a 0.035 safety J guidewire through the needle. The needle is removed, leaving the guidewire in the artery.
- The provided dilator is slid over the wire and into the artery to dilate a passageway for the balloon. Leaving the guidewire in place, the dilator is removed, with pressure applied to the arterial puncture site to prevent bleeding.
- The sheath/dilator is inserted over the guidewire and slid into the artery up to the skin line, using a rotary motion to facilitate its passage.
- Connect the provided 60 ml syringe to the one-way valve after connecting the valve to the male luer end of the balloon.
- Aspirate 60 ml of air and remove the syringe, leaving the valve in position.
- The patient should now be anticoagulated with heparin.
- After lubricating the balloon tip with sterile saline, remove the inner stylet from the balloon. Remove the dilator from the sheath, which is in the femoral artery, pinching the sheath around the guidewire to minimize blood loss.
- The balloon is then inserted over the guidewire until the wire exits the female luer fitting of the balloon. The balloon is advanced into the sheath and up to the desired position in the descending aorta, just distal to the left subclavian artery.
- The guidewire is then removed; blood is aspirated from the balloon lumen, which is then attached to a standard arterial pressure-monitoring transducer. The one-way valve is removed, and the male luer fitting is attached to the balloon console safety chamber; balloon pumping may now be initiated.
- The sheath is sutured to the skin to prevent dislodgement. It is essential to ensure that the balloon has fully exited the sheath before pumping is initiated, and its optimum position should be established radiologically.

● The timing of inflation and deflation is adjusted on the balloon pump console to augment peak diastolic pressure optimally.

Complications

Complications include:

● trauma to the aortic wall;
● limb ischaemia, which may require removal of the balloon if it cannot be resolved; and
● sepsis.

INTUBATION

● **Pharyngeal intubation:** in the deeply unconscious patient, oro-pharyngeal airway tubes prevent obstruction to ventilation from the lips and teeth, in addition to holding the base of the tongue forward.

● *Technique*: the tube is inserted with the concave aspect facing the hard palate. Rotating it 180° places the tip behind the base of the tongue in the laryngopharynx, and the head should be extended by backward tilt.

There are S-shaped tubes available to allow air to be breathed into the patient without the need for mouth-to-mouth contact: the patient's nose being pinched closely with the operator's thumbs to prevent air leakage, whilst the mandible is held forward with the fingers. Observation of chest-wall movement allows an assessment of adequacy of ventilation.

An alternative is the pocket mask: this is held tightly against the patient's face with the thumbs, and the mandible is pulled forwards and the mouth opened with the fingers. The operator inflates the lungs with expired air, observing chest-wall movement; as with the S-tube, expiration occurs passively through the device. With some of these masks there is an oxygen inlet port to allow ventilation with oxygen.

● **Endotracheal intubation:** this technique completely isolates the airway, protecting it in unconscious patients, and allowing adequate ventilation. The patient should be supine, with the head tilted back. In the elderly, who may have cervical spinal arthritis, care must be taken not to over-extend the neck, which can result in spinal damage.

- *Technique*: unconscious patients usually do not require drug therapy prior to intubation, but some may require a short-acting intravenous anaesthetic.

The following equipment will be needed:

- Sterile disposable endotracheal tubes of the correct size: in general an adult male will require a 9.0−9.5 mm diameter tube; adult females usually require 8.0−8.5 mm tubes. The length of tube required may be estimated by placing it alongside the patient's face and neck: the carina lies at the level of the manubrio sternal joint, and the tube may need to be cut if time allows for this. A blunt introducer is useful in difficult intubations to exert some control over the tube curve, but should not protrude beyond the end of the endotracheal tube.

- A laryngoscope with a curved blade (Macintosh); this is designed to fit in the vallecula just above the epiglottis.

- A syringe is needed to inflate the cuff.

- Artery forceps will be required to seal the cuff.

- A bandage is needed to hold the tube in place.

- Adaptors and a connecting tube are required to connect the endotracheal tube to ventilation equipment.

- A self-refilling bag is needed with, at one end, a one-way inlet valve to which an oxygen supply can be connected. A non-rebreathing valve is attached to the other end, which connects to the endotracheal tube or mask.

Difficulty with intubation may result from patients' having short, thick necks, protruding teeth, or cervical spinal arthritis, or from their being conscious.

Following the removal of any dentures, the laryngoscope should be introduced, held in the left hand, into the right corner of the mouth, pushing the tongue to the left when moved into the midline. Passage of the laryngoscope posteriorly into the vallecula allows visualization of the epiglottis. Lifting forward the laryngoscope usually exposes the vocal cords. Great care must be taken to avoid damage to the teeth; and in particular the operator must avoid levering the laryngoscope against the upper teeth.

Stimulation of the pharynx may result in vomiting, and suction should be available for this eventuality. The lumen of the oesophagus can be occluded by an assistant's pressing the cricoid cartilage backwards until the tube is in place, and this can prevent vomitus reaching the laryngopharyngeal area.

Insertion of the endotracheal tube may be facilitated by an assistant's retracting the right corner of the patient's mouth, thereby improving visibility for the operator. The assistant should maintain pressure on the cricoid cartilage whilst the tube is advanced through the vocal cords. It is positioned with the cuff just below the larynx, and the cuff is inflated until there is no air leak heard on ventilation, at which point the cuff pressure is sufficient. The artery forceps are applied proximal to the pressure-limiting balloon seal (which is an indicator that the cuff is not over- or underinflated).

If there is spontaneous respiration, the chest should be observed for symmetrical movement, and auscultated for an assessment of air entry. If ventilation is required, a connecting tube is positioned between the endotracheal tube and the ventilation equipment. With the patient under ventilation the chest is observed and auscultated to ensure that the tube is positioned correctly. If the tube has been inserted too far it may have entered the right main bronchus, and there will be right-sided chest-inflation only: the tube should be withdrawn (with the cuff deflated) until equal air entry bilaterally is achieved. If the chest does not move with ventilation and air entry is not heard, consider the possibility that the tube is in the oesophagus: this leads to gastric dilatation, and, of course, is not associated with gas exchange; and the tube must be repositioned immediately. Once a satisfactory position has been obtained, a bandage should be placed around the tube and around the neck to limit the potential for dislodgement. Finally, an oropharyngeal airway should be inserted to prevent the patient's biting and occluding the tube.

● **Bag and oxygen ventilation:** whilst awaiting endotracheal intubation or should intubation fail, the patient should receive ventilatory assistance via a well-fitting mask held tightly against the face with the head tilted backwards. With an airway in position, the mask is placed over the mouth and nose, with one hand being used to maintain a tight seal. The thumb and index finger are used to anchor the mask, whilst the other fingers are used to pull the mandible upwards and forwards. The free hand squeezes the bag, with careful observation of chest-wall movement to ensure adequate ventilation. Exhalation occurs through the valve on release of the bag pressure.

PACING

The indications for cardiac pacing are described under **cardiac arrhythmias** in Chapter 6. These include symptomatic sino-atrial disease, complete heart block complicating inferior infarction with haemodynamic disturbance, and complete heart block in anterior infarction. After myocardial infarction, pacing should be considered in patients with right-bundle branch-block and an abnormal axis; in patients developing left-bundle branch-block; and in those with Mobitz type II block, particularly if the PR interval is prolonged.

Preparation for pacing

Sedation is rarely needed, but the patient should be as comfortable as possible, with a single pillow supporting the head.

The pacing trolley should contain:

- large, sterile towels;
- an iodine skin preparation, or an alternative for patients with iodine allergy;
- a Seldinger introducer needle;
- a short safety J guidewire;
- an introducer sheath (better if haemostatic);
- heparinized saline as a flush solution;
- a bipolar pacing electrode; and
- a sterile cable to connect the pacing electrode to the external generator.

Subclavian or femoral route?

There are advantages to employing the subclavian venous route for temporary pacing: the vein is relatively easy to enter, and the pacing electrode can be more easily immobilized and cared for than is possible using femoral venous pacing, allowing the patient to be mobile. The femoral approach should be used if sufficient experience with the subclavian route is not available; it is safer, and of course it should be used as the route of choice if the patient is about to receive, or has received, thrombolysis, to avoid uncontrollable bleeding. The femoral route should also be preferred in severe airways disease, where a pneumothorax would be a threatening development.

Subclavian vein cannulation

The subclavian vein provides an ideal conduit for the insertion of pacing electrodes and Swan–Ganz (balloon-flotation) catheters and for rapid fluid replacement. Even in patients with collapsed circulation it is usually easily entered with experience.

It is important to recognize, however, that important adjacent structures, including nerves and the artery, can be damaged, as this procedure is performed by a blind stab without visualizing the vein. This procedure should only be performed, then, by experienced staff or under close supervision.

The subclavian vein lies in the angle between the middle third of the clavicle and the first rib.

The patient should be supine or in the head-down position. (This increases the size of the vein by means of increased venous return, and also minimizes the possibility of air embolization.)

Either side may be used, although, if patients have sustained a fractured clavicle at some time, that side should be avoided. A sterile technique must be employed, using appropriate surface antiseptic and towelling. A wide area (to include the clavicle and suprasternal notch), should be prepared so that the surface markings can be palpated without compromising sterility.

The mid-point of the clavicle (Figs. 8.1 and 8.2) should be identified, in addition to the suprasternal notch. Local anaesthetic is inserted in the skin immediately below the mid-point of the clavicle, and into the tissues in the proposed course of the introducing needle.

When anaesthesia has been obtained, a 6 French cannula is inserted by placing the introducer needle as horizontally as possible under the clavicle. The index finger of the other hand should apply pressure to the end of the needle so that it can be guided under the clavicle without the need for posterior pointing, reducing the likelihood of pneumothorax.

The needle (placed on a syringe and filled with saline) should be advanced aiming towards the suprasternal notch; and it is quite useful to place a finger in the notch at which to aim (Fig. 8.3). The needle should be advanced under suction until venous blood is aspirated, whereupon the needle should be inserted slightly further to ensure that the needle is in the vein, and not just part of the bevel.

A guidewire is inserted through the needle along the subclavian vein and into the superior vena cava under radiological control (Fig. 8.4).

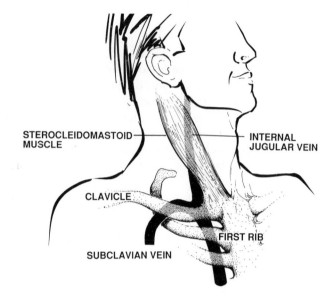

Fig. 8.1 Subclavian vein cannulation: anatomy.

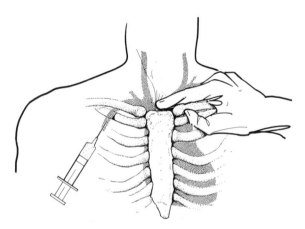

Fig. 8.2 Subclavian venous puncture.

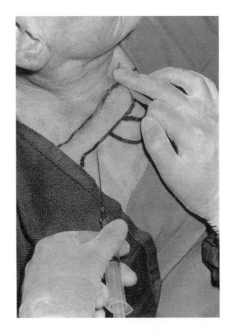

Fig. 8.3 Approach to the subclavian vein.

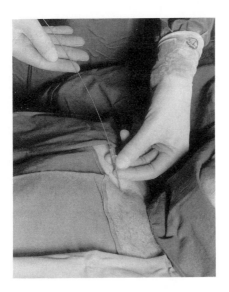

Fig. 8.4 Guidewire insertion.

The sheath must not be introduced if there is a possibility that the artery has been punctured, as this would increase the size of the arterial wall puncture. It should be possible to establish that the vein has been entered: venous blood is usually more desaturated in appearance, and arterial blood is pulsatile. Unwell patients may have desaturated arterial blood, however, and in right heart failure venous blood may be under impressive back pressure. Furthermore, an inadvertent arterial puncture causes the guidewire to impinge on the aortic valve, and it is good practice in this situation to pass the guidewire down into the right atrium to ensure that the superior vena cava has been accessed. The needle is removed, and the appropriate-sized cannula (French 6 for a French 6 pacing electrode), is inserted on a dilator over the guidewire, rotating it as it is advanced to facilitate entry (Fig. 8.5). Care should be taken to immobilize the guidewire so that it is not lost into the vein. Once the guidewire is removed, it is good practice to occlude the unoccupied end of the cannula with a finger to further limit the possibility of air aspiration, until the electrode is inserted (Fig. 8.6).

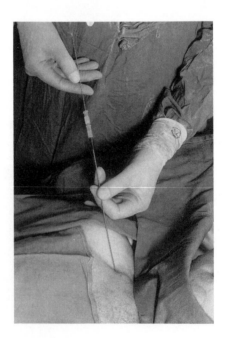

Fig. 8.5 Cannula insertion.

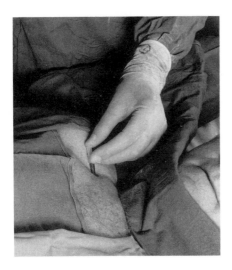

Fig. 8.6 Care should be taken to avoid aspiration of air.

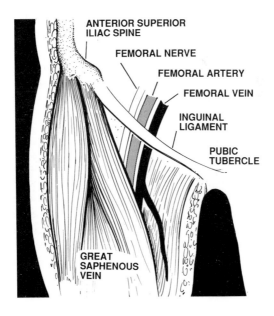

ANTERIOR SUPERIOR
ILIAC SPINE

FEMORAL NERVE

FEMORAL ARTERY

FEMORAL VEIN

INGUINAL
LIGAMENT

PUBIC
TUBERCLE

GREAT
SAPHENOUS
VEIN

Fig. 8.7 Femoral vein cannulation: anatomy.

Femoral vein cannulation

This is perhaps the easiest, and therefore the safest, route for in-experienced operators.

The vein lies medial to the artery, which is itself medial to the femoral nerve (Fig. 8.7). The artery is easily palpated at the level of the inguinal ligament, and the vein lies about a finger's breadth medially.

It may be helpful to palpate the femoral artery between the index and middle fingers, pointing down the patient's leg: when the operator's fingers are together, the vein should then lie under the middle finger. The introducer needle should approach the vein at an angle of approximately 45°: this increases the potential cross-sectional area of the target vein, increasing the likelihood of a successful puncture.

If the attempt is unsuccessful, remove the needle and ensure haemostasis by pressure over the puncture site: if a haematoma is allowed to develop it will make subsequent attempts more difficult. Multiple fruitless attempts should not be permitted, and a more experienced operator should be summoned in this eventuality. If thrombolysis has been administered and pacing is deemed essential, the most experienced operator available should insert the pacing electrode, to limit the potential for haemorrhage.

Venous puncture is confirmed by aspiration of desaturated blood which is not pulsatile (although in right-heart failure, venous flow may be impressive). In addition, the subsequent course of the pacing electrode is to the right of the spine if the vein has been entered.

Positioning of the electrode

The guidewire and dilator are removed, and care should be taken to avoid air aspiration whilst the cannula lumen is unoccupied (by placing a finger over the end of the cannula). The pacing electrode is then inserted, and under radiological control is advanced into the right ventricle and positioned, ideally with its tip pointing inferiorly and with a gentle curve in its course through the right atrium to facilitate a stable position (Fig. 8.8). If difficulty is experienced in accessing the right ventricle, placing the electrode tip in the right atrium with a curve pointing away from the tricuspid valve often allows success when the electrode is rotated through 180° using the finger and thumb (rather than the wrist).

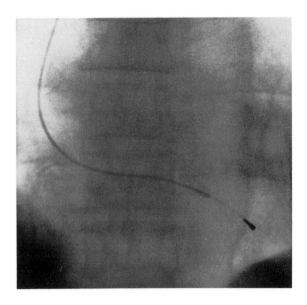

Fig. 8.8 Right ventricular endocardial electrode position on screening.

Crossing the tricuspid valve is often accompanied by arrhythmias (so often, that it serves as a marker of the proximity of the electrode to the valve); if the procedure produces sustained arrhythmias, however, the manoeuvre should be suspended temporarily to allow the ventricular irritability to settle.

Difficulty crossing the tricuspid valve is often solved by removing the electrode and reshaping the curve of the tip, usually to a lesser degree. A common problem experienced, and unrecognized, by the inexperienced operator is entry of the electrode into the coronary sinus; this results in the electrode's being directed upwards and to the left at the patient's left shoulder. The electrode appears to be in the right ventricle; but reliable pacing with an acceptable threshold will often be unobtainable. If a lateral image is available it will be clear if the coronary sinus has been entered, as the electrode is angled in a posterior direction, whereas an electrode in the right ventricle is directed anteriorly. Finally, electrodes which are positioned correctly, pointing downwards and to the left, are never in the coronary sinus.

At no time should force be used when positioning pacing or monitoring devices, as it is possible to penetrate the myocardium, which in the right ventricle is relatively thin, especially in the elderly, or if the right ventricle is involved in the infarction.

Measuring the threshold

The pacing electrode is connected to an external generator using the cable provided. An acceptable electrical position is obtained by establishing the threshold—the minimum energy required to achieve reliable pacing of the ventricle using an external generator. The ventricle is paced at 10 beats above the patient's own rate, and the voltage amplitude (energy) is reduced until capture is lost.

An attempt should be made to find a threshold of one volt (or 1mA) or less. Because of the likelihood of a rise in the pacing threshold after the procedure, the generator should be set at 1 volt above the threshold level, and this should be assessed daily. High energy levels should be avoided in myocardial ischaemia, to reduce the possibility of triggering serious arrhythmias; an increase in the threshold, requiring high-energy pacing, raises the possibility that the electrode has moved or perforated, and repositioning should be considered.

The electrode must be anchored to the skin, to prevent movement of the electrode and the loss of pacing capture.

Finally, covering the pacing site with a clear, occlusive dressing allows the site to be kept clean, further reduces mobility of the electrode, and allows frequent visualization of the wound site to detect early signs of sepsis.

After pacing

In a pacemaker-dependent patient, if pacing capture is lost, immediately check all the connections. If no cause for the failure is discovered, increase the pacing output. Reversal of the pacing lead connections attached to the pacing generator may restore pacing. This development suggests movement of the endocardial electrode, which must be repositioned as soon as possible. If, in order to achieve this, an unsterile electrode would be inserted into the vein, a new electrode should be placed using a different site, though one should always be mindful to protect the site which may be required for permanent pacing, which is usually a subclavian approach.

The pacing threshold should be checked daily to lessen the possibility of an acute, unrecognized rise in pacing threshold, which might allow loss of capture. The routine use of antibiotics for uncomplicated insertion of a temporary pacing electrode is not recommended. Pacing-site infections should be vigorously treated, however, and the presumed agent would be *Staphylococcus epidermidis*.

The pacing site should be inspected daily, and the system should be replaced at the first sign of infection, the electrode tip and blood cultures being sent for bacteriological analysis.

These electrodes should probably not be left in position for more than five days: if there is a continued need for temporary pacing, they should be replaced using an alternative site, reserving a subclavian approach for a permanent pacing procedure if required.

Non-invasive pacing

For the urgent pacing of patients with asystole or profound brady-cardia, external transthoracic pacing is available. The advantage of this technique is that it is comparatively simple, and requires minimal training, so that non-cardiac physicians, nurses, and paramedics can institute temporary pacing, thereby buying time or supporting the circulation until transvenous pacing can be performed. This form of pacing can be performed almost immediately, avoiding the preparation and insertion time associated with invasive techniques. Non-invasive pacing has an attractive role to play where invasive techniques might be contraindicated or especially hazardous, as in patients with systemic infection or bleeding tendencies, or where thrombolysis has been or is likely to be administered. Finally, this form of pacing can be used as standby prophylaxis: it may be useful, for example, where there is an uncertain potential for heart block, as in patients undergoing surgery who have conduction disturbances that would conventionally require the prophylactic insertion of an electrode that may never be needed.

The technique involves placing electrodes preferably in the antero-posterior position on the chest wall—the negative electrode on the left anterior chest half-way between the xiphoid process and the left nipple, the upper edge of the electrode being below the nipple line. The positive electrode is positioned on the left posterior chest, beneath the scapula and lateral to the spine. During pacing skeletal muscle con-traction should be expected, and does not indicate pacing capture.

Patients experience 'tingles, twitches, thudding, and tapping', varying from the tolerable to the intolerable.

PERICARDIAL ASPIRATION

This may be indicated in haemodynamically compromised patients who have been shown by cardiac ultrasound to have large pericardial effusions. It may also be indicated in patients with well-tolerated effusions in the search for a diagnosis; but it should be recognized that the likelihood of obtaining diagnostic information is surprisingly low, at about 20 per cent.

Technique

- Explain the procedure to the patient, obtain his or her consent, and, if indicated, premedicate the patient with appropriate sedation.
- Use a sterile technique with mask, gloves, gown, and sterile drapes.
- Position the patient sitting up at 45°, and prepare the puncture site with antiseptic to which the patient is not allergic. The patient should be connected to a cardiac monitor.
- Infiltrate the skin and tissues of the proposed needle track with 1 per cent lignocaine, aspirating before every infiltration.
- Pericardial aspiration sets are commercially produced; but if one is not available use a 14-gauge needle and cannula attached to a syringe via a three-way tap; the V lead of an ECG machine should be attached, using a sterile crocodile clip, to the proximal part of the needle—should the myocardium be breached a current of injury (ST elevation) will alert the operator to withdraw the needle.

Xiphisternal approach

This is the safest and therefore the preferred route. The needle should be introduced between the xiphoid process and the left costal margin, aiming towards the left shoulder at 15° to the horizontal plane and 15° to the sagittal plane.

Apical approach

Introduce the needle in the fourth or fifth intercostal space 2 cm medial to the lateral edge of the cardiac dullness. There is an increased risk of trauma to the coronary arteries using this route.

Using either technique

● Insert the needle slowly on suction, so that entry to the pericardium can be detected promptly. Many pericardial aspirates will be heavily bloodstained; but clearly consideration has to be given to the possibility that a cardiac chamber has been entered: in general, a failure of the aspirated 'blood' to clot in a container suggests that it is not whole blood, but a bloodstained aspirate. Many operators will attempt aspiration under ultrasound control, allowing more confidence that the pericardial space has been entered. If there continues to be doubt, angiographic contrast can be administered down the cannula: under screening, if the cannula lies in the pericardium the contrast will settle and remain at the most dependent level. Any contrast injected into the circulation will be rapidly (and safely) whisked away.

● Once the pericardium has been entered, the needle should be removed to lessen the potential for cardiac contusion, and further aspiration should be made through the plastic cannula. If a dedicated aspiration set is available, once the pericardial space has been entered with confidence, a guidewire is inserted through the needle and into the pericardial space. With the wire anchored in place, the needle is removed and the plastic (and therefore less traumatic) cannula is advanced over the wire and into the pericardial space. Once again contrast may be used to confirm correct positioning of the cannula. Finally, removal of the guidewire allows aspiration of pericardial contents, and the cannula may be left *in situ* for continuous drainage if rapid reaccumulation is anticipated. The cannula should then be secured to the skin (but not so tightly that the lumen of the cannula is constricted).

● Following aspiration, an X-ray should be performed to exclude the possibility of pneumothorax.

● Frequent observations should be performed (pulse and blood-pressure quarter-hourly for two hours, half-hourly for two hours, and then four-hourly until it is established that the patient is haemodynamically stable).

● Slowly reaccumulating effusions may be managed best by leaving a soft cannula in the pericardium to drain continuously; a rapidly reaccumulating effusion, however, raises the possibility of a traumatic effusion that requires urgent surgical intervention.

● Pericardial aspiration is a potentially hazardous procedure, and should only be performed by or under the supervision of an experienced member of staff: perforation of the right ventricle, arrhythmias, and coronary arterial laceration may occur.

SWAN–GANZ CATHETERIZATION

These pressure-monitoring catheters are inserted in patients with complicated infarction in whom a knowledge of the intracardiac pressures might allow a change in therapy with benefit: patients with hypotension may be either hypovolaemic or have pump failure, and haemodynamic monitoring will discriminate between them. It will also allow the effect of any therapy to be monitored closely, so that appropriate action may be taken early, before the development of signs.

The catheters are inserted in a manner similar to that of pacing electrode insertion (see **pacing** above), and a size 6 or 7 is usually employed.

The tip of the catheter contains an inflatable balloon, which allows the catheter to be flow-directed to the appropriate chamber. The fluid-filled catheter is attached to a pressure transducer, so that after calibration reliable intracardiac pressure-monitoring can be performed.

Technique

The integrity of the balloon should be tested before insertion by injecting the recommended volume of air into the balloon port and then deflating it. Following insertion the catheter is advanced to the right atrium and the balloon is inflated. The catheter usually floats up into the pulmonary artery with little difficulty, and appropriate progress is identified by changes in the pressure waveform if the catheter is connected to a pressure transducer. The catheter is advanced under radiological control if available (by observing appropriate pressure change if not), to the pulmonary artery (see Fig. 8.9a–d for examples of pressure changes). Advancing the catheter more distally into the

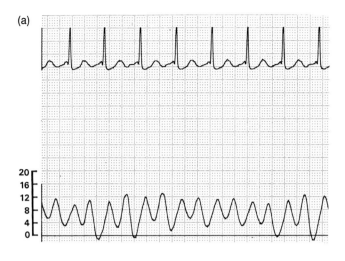

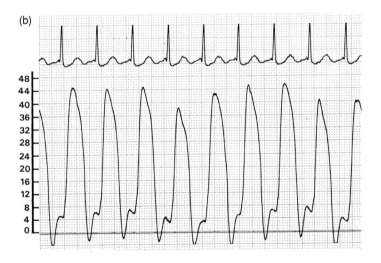

Fig. 8.9 (a). Right atrial pressure. (b). Right ventricular pressure. (c). Pulmonary artery pressure. (d). Pulmonary wedge pressure.

Continued overleaf

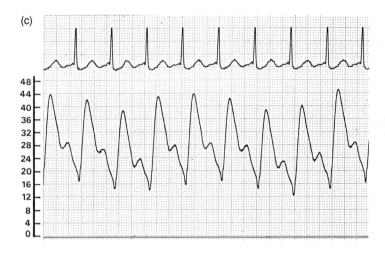

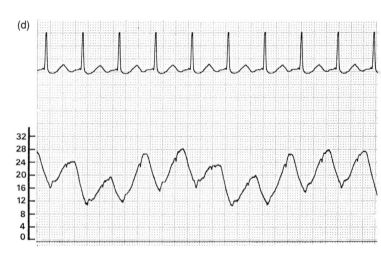

Fig. 8.9 *continued.*

pulmonary artery and gently inflating the balloon (the full volume may not be needed) should allow measurement of the mean pulmonary wedge pressure, which in the absence of severe airways disease is closely related to the left atrial pressure. Deflation (the balloon must not be left inflated) then gives the pulmonary artery pressure.

Catheters are available which also have a lumen for simultaneous right atrial pressure measurement. Additionally, catheters may have a thermistor, which allows calculation of the cardiac output by thermo-dilution when used with an appropriate cardiac output computer.

With appropriate attention to sepsis these catheters can be left *in situ* for several days to allow repeated measurements to be made, but must be removed at the first sign of infection, the catheter tip being sent for bacteriological analysis.

Normal resting right heart pressures

- right atrium   0–5 (mean 3) mm Hg;
- pulmonary artery   20–30/5–13 mm Hg;
- pulmonary wedge   5–12 (mean) mm Hg;
- cardiac index   2.5–4.1/min/m^2.

VENFLON INSERTION

A 17G or 18G Venflon should be selected, and an appropriate vein should be identified. GTN ointment may allow dilatation of hard-to-cannulate veins.

- The operator must ensure that a sterile technique is employed that includes a proper hand-scrub technique.

- The venous access site should be prepared with iodine, or an alternative skin antiseptic if the patient has a known iodine hypersensitivity. Hairs may need to be shaved carefully, avoiding abrading the skin.

- Efforts should be made to prevent movement of the cannula by inserting the Venflon up to its hilt, thus reducing the potential for infection. An occlusive dressing further protects the puncture site and limits the possibility of unwanted movement.

- It is recommended that these cannulae are replaced daily in patients with valvular heart disease, because of the risk of endocarditis.

● Daily inspection of the venous site is essential, and any clinical evidence of infection requires removal of the cannula; and in this eventuality the cannula tip and blood cultures should be sent for bacteriological analysis.

X-RAY SCREENING

Most units will have access to an image-intensifier for the purpose of inserting pacing electrodes and monitoring catheters. It is now a requirement that this equipment is used only by those who have attended a course in radiological safety. The operator and other staff present must wear lead protection at all times when X-ray screening is being used. There are no exceptions to this, and staff who are not actively involved in the procedure should stand away from the patient, as the X-ray scatter diminishes impressively with distance from the X-ray source. The intensifier should be as close to the patient as possible, to restrict X-ray scatter. Operators should attempt to keep their hands out of the X-ray field, and only image when looking at the screen: it is poor medical practice to maintain screening inadvertently whilst the images obtained are being ignored, as this merely exposes the patient, staff, and the operator to harmful X-rays. Radiation monitor badges should be worn under the lead protection, so that an assessment can be made of the total radiation level to which any member of staff is exposed.

9

Cardiac drugs

Caution: calculating the correct dosage of parenteral agents prescribed according to patient weight is difficult and liable to error. Do use the wall charts or pocket aids provided by manufacturers for this purpose.

Inotropic agents should be avoided in patients with obstructive valve disease or with hypertrophic cardiomyopathy: they may result in a deleterious increase in the pressure gradient.

ADENOSINE

This endogenous nucleoside is capable of causing atrioventricular nodal conduction block when injected intravenously. It is rapidly becoming the treatment of choice for the termination of paroxysmal supraventricular tachycardia with re-entry circuits that include the atrioventricular node. In addition to this useful therapeutic role it also has a valuable diagnostic contribution to make. The misdiagnosis of broad-complex arrhythmias is common, and may have serious sequelae if inappropriate therapy is administered as a consequence. By terminating most junctional tachycardias (whether there is aberration or not) and by producing AV nodal block, which will reveal intra-atrial arrhythmias but have no effect on ventricular arrhythmias, adenosine is useful in the diagnostic separation of these arrhythmias. The extreme brevity of action of adenosine (half life less than two seconds) allows a conclusion that adenosine is safe and of value as a diagnostic test in cases of broad-complex, regular tachycardia in which the diagnosis remains uncertain after analysis of the 12-lead electrocardiogram (Rankin *et al.* 1989).

Indications for adenosine therapy are:

- narrow-complex, regular tachycardia when there is doubt as to whether it is atrial or junctional;
- junctional tachycardia when there is evidence of impaired ventricular function or concomitant beta-blockade; and

- as a diagnostic tool in patients with well-tolerated, regular, broad-complex tachycardia when the ECG suggests a supraventricular origin or is inconclusive.

Adenosine is not recommended in patients with irregular tachycardia.

Dosage: 3 mg by rapid intravenous injection. If this is unsuccessful a further bolus of 6 mg should be administered. If this does not result in a favourable clinical outcome, a 12 mg bolus should be administered.

Adverse effects: Patients should be warned about transient chest discomfort, dyspnoea, and flushing, usually lasting less than a minute, which are common but usually well tolerated.

AMIODARONE

This agent, which prolongs the action potential, is very successful in the control of both supraventricular and ventricular arrhythmias. It is largely reserved for threatening and complex arrhythmias or for those which have proven refractory to other antiarrhythmic agents.

Oral therapy only achieves benefit after about six days, and is therefore only for chronic management of rhythm disturbances. Intravenous therapy results in rapid activity. Another problem relates to the long elimination half life of some 45 days, so that antiarrhythmic and toxic effects can continue for weeks after therapy is discontinued.

Dosage: *intravenously* 5 mg/kg over 20 minutes in emergencies or over 2–4 hours if time allows, with a total of 1200 mg in 24 hours. It is desirable to administer IV amiodarone via a central line to prevent the phlebitis which may complicate its use into peripheral lines.

Dosage: *orally* 200 mg four times daily for a week and then 200 mg daily (increasing if control is not achieved), to minimize adverse effects, which are dose-related and relatively infrequent at doses below 400 mg daily.

Adverse effects:

- photosensitivity, causing impressive blue pigmentation in patients exposed to the sun—patients should be cautioned to use **complete** sun blockers;
- either hypo- or hyperthyroidism;
- abnormal liver function;
- pulmonary alveolitis, particularly in patients with previous lung disease;

- more rarely, metallic taste, nausea, headache, sleeplessness, vertigo, nightmares, fatigue, and ataxia;
- enhancement of anticoagulant effect; and
- increased concentration of digoxin due to interference with digoxin metabolism—digoxin dosage should be halved if it is used in combination with amiodarone.

Therefore this agent should not be considered lightly; therapy with other agents should be attempted first in most circumstances, and if possible measurements of baseline liver, thyroid, and pulmonary function should be performed before beginning amiodarone therapy.

ANGIOTENSIN-CONVERTING ENZYME (ACE) INHIBITORS

These agents act as useful vasodilators, which exert favourable effects on elevated blood-pressure and in cardiac failure by reducing vascular resistance. The renin–angiotensin system is considerably active in the presence of cardiac failure. The result is angiotensin-related vasoconstriction and aldosterone-mediated salt and water retention. By preventing the conversion of the relatively inactive angiotensin I to angiotensin II, a potent vasoconstrictor which also stimulates production of aldosterone, ACE inhibitors exert their favourable effects in cardiac failure, resulting in increased cardiac output and less fluid retention.

After myocardial infarction, these agents may prevent the unfavourable remodelling and infarct expansion that is often associated with late complications. The SAVE trial investigators have shown that, in patients with asymptomatic left ventricular dysfunction after myocardial infarction, long-term captopril therapy was associated with improved survival and reduced cardiovascular morbidity (Pfeffer *et al.* 1992).

Dosage: captopril 6.25 mg three times daily; and, if tolerated, this can be increased stepwise to 25 mg three times daily, according to benefit.

A change to a long acting ACE inhibitor such as **lisinopril** or **enalapril** (20 mg daily if on captopril 25 mg three times daily) allows a reduction in the number of tablets. No potassium supplementation is usually required with these potassium-sparing agents.

Adverse effects: The adverse effects of these agents include rash, taste disturbance, and hypotension. Some patients also experience a troublesome cough, which can be ignored if it is tolerated by the patient.

They may give rise to excessive hypotension in patients with sodium depletion resulting from diuretic therapy. They may also be associated with deteriorating renal function in patients with renal artery stenosis. Patients should be supine for the first two hours after the initial dose, to reduce the possibility of postural hypotension; and a small initial dose should be employed. Renal function should be assessed before treatment and repeated after patients are established on treatment to identify the albeit unlikely possibility of renal dysfunction developing in patients with undiagnosed renal artery stenosis.

ASPIRIN

By inhibiting thromboxane, which causes platelet aggregation, aspirin acts to prevent blood coagulation. It has been shown to reduce mortality after infarction both used alone and combined with thrombolysis. It has also been shown to reduce the incidence of both infarction and mortality in patients with unstable angina.

Dosage: 150 mg per day (used crushed or dissolved in acute infarction for earlier bioavailability).

ATROPINE

Atropine antagonizes vagal stimulation and is helpful in increasing heart rate where bradycardia results in haemodynamic disturbance. It may result in drowsiness, a dry mouth, urinary retention, or blurred vision which are reversible. It is contraindicated in glaucoma.

Dosage: 600–1200 micrograms intravenously.

BETA-BLOCKERS

In addition to their favourable effects on myocardial ischaemia and hypertension, these agents have beneficial antiarrhythmic properties, but are more usually employed in the management of supraventricular rhythm disturbances. They may also usefully control the rate of atrial fibrillation when digoxin is unsuitable or unsuccessful. They have been shown to reduce cardiac mortality and further non-fatal infarction after myocardial infarction.

Dosage: *IV* **propranolol** (non-selective): 1 mg; repeated up to 5 mg.
Dosage: *oral* **propranolol:** 120−360 mg per day in divided doses.

Dosage: *IV* **metoprolol** (cardioselective): 5 mg over 2 minutes repeated up to a total of 15 mg.
Dosage: *oral* **metoprolol:** 50−100 mg three times daily.

Dosage: *IV* **atenolol** (cardioselective and long-acting): 5−10 mg over 5 minutes.
Dosage: *oral* **atenolol:** 50−100 mg daily.

Their use should be avoided in cardiac failure (they are significantly negatively inotropic), in patients with heart block, in those with asthma (risk of bronchospasm), and in patients with peripheral vascular disease (risk of vasoconstriction). (This last is only a relative contraindication, and the benefits of beta-blockade should not be withheld unless the peripheral circulatory problem is advanced and threatening.)

BRETYLIUM

This agent inhibits release of noradrenaline from sympathetic neurones and prolongs the action potential. It may be useful in the management of resistant ventricular arrhythmias.

It takes at least 10 minutes to exert a clinical effect, and, during a cardiac arrest, resuscitation should be continued for at least this period. It is recommended for the management of life-threatening arrhythmias which fail to respond to either lignocaine or procainamide. In addition, ventricular fibrillation that fails to respond to repeated direct-current countershock may respond to bretylium and countershock.

Dosage: 5 mg/kg in 50 ml 5 per cent dextrose over 10 minutes intravenously. Maintenance is with 1−2 mg/minute. Dosages should be reduced in patients with renal disease.

Adverse effects: These include nausea and vomiting; orthostatic hypotension is also common, and if this is a significant problem in supine patients, fluid expansion will usually resolve it.

CALCIUM ANTAGONISTS

These agents selectively inhibit the slow inward calcium current in vascular smooth muscle and in nodal tissue. Verapamil, nifedipine, and diltiazem each have a slightly different spectrum of clinical effects; but they all result in vasodilation.

● **Verapamil:** this calcium-channel blocker, in addition to its anti-hypertensive and anti-anginal properties, has antiarrhythmic effects also through its action on the AV node. It is particularly useful in the management of supraventricular tachycardia, which is usually due to a re-entry mechanism.

By slowing the ventricular response in atrial fibrillation and flutter, it is helpful in managing these arrhythmias as an alternative to digoxin.

It is available both orally and intravenously, but its bioavailability is poor, at about 25 per cent, owing to its extensive hepatic first-pass metabolism.

Dosage: *IV*: 5−10 mg over 30 seconds.

Dosage: *oral*: 40−120 mg three times daily.

Adverse effects: It does have negative inotropic effects, and caution should be exercised in patients with cardiac failure, and it should be avoided in patients with or at risk of heart block. In particular the combination of verapamil and beta-blockers can result in extreme bradycardia, and the combination should not be used intravenously. Verapamil may be associated with troublesome constipation in chronic oral usage.

● **Nifedipine:** this dihydropyridine is a powerful arterial dilator with little effect on the AV node. It is useful in the management of hypertension and angina (especially related to vasospasm), but is not effective in the management of arrhythmias; but its combination with beta-blockers is theoretically less hazardous than is the case with verapamil or diltiazem.

Dosage: *oral*: 10−20 mg three times daily.

Adverse effects: These include flushing and ankle oedema, both of which are usually trivial, and a mild reflex tachycardia which may be undesirable in myocardial ischaemia.

● **Diltiazem:** this agent has similar clinical indications to verapamil, having inhibitory effects on the AV node. It does appear to have a relatively clean side-effect profile, and is usually well tolerated.

Dosage: 180−360 mg in three divided doses.

These agents have not been shown convincingly to reduce mortality after infarction, as does beta-blockade (Muller *et al.* 1984). However, diltiazem has been shown to improve survival, possibly, in patients with non-Q wave infarction (Gibson *et al.* 1986).

CYCLIZINE

An antiemetic should be administered with any opiate given to relieve cardiac pain. Cyclizine can be administered with diamorphine intravenously in the dose of 50 mg; in the presence of left ventricular failure or shock **metoclopramide** 10 mg should be used instead, because of the tendency of cyclizine to increase peripheral resistance—but not mixed with the diamorphine.

DIAMORPHINE

Opiates exert favourable effects by being analgesic and anxiolytic, and they have desirable vasodilatory properties in addition, whereby they reduce pulmonary congestion. Diamorphine 2.5–5.0 mg should be used intravenously at 1 mg per minute, in addition to increments of 2.5 mg at 10-minute intervals until pain is relieved. The opiates may result in hypotension resulting from their vasodilatory effects, and they may also be associated with respiratory depression, especially in patients with airways disease, in whom a smaller dose should be administered in small increments. Any respiratory depression may be reversed with **naloxone** (0.8 mg intravenously), and this may need to be repeated after five minutes to a maximum of 10 mg, remembering that the analgesic effects of the opiate will also be reversed.

Cyclizine 50 mg should also be used to limit the associated nausea, and both should be given intravenously, to achieve a rapid and reliable response, but also to reduce the possibility of confounding enzyme release from skeletal muscle that may interfere with subsequent diagnosis. In the presence of shock or left ventricular failure **metoclopramide** 10 mg should be employed, to avoid the potential constrictor properties of cyclizine.

DIGOXIN

This agent inhibits the action of Na^+/K^+ ATPase, thereby inhibiting the sodium pump. It has inotropic effects, and also slows the ventricular rate in atrial fibrillation. The former effect may be undesirable in acute myocardial ischaemia, because of the associated rise in myocardial oxygen consumption. It has a narrow therapeutic–toxic ratio and some caution should be exercised in its use: not all patients with atrial fibrillation require therapy, particularly if the rate is slow or the arrhythmia is well tolerated.

Digoxin should be avoided in WPW pre-excitation, where it can speed conduction in the bypass tract.

Dosage: *IV*: 0.5–1.0 mg in 100 ml of 5 per cent dextrose over at least 30 minutes.

Dosage: *oral*: 1 mg loading dose in the first 24 hours in divided doses; 0.25 mg daily thereafter. The dose should be reduced in the elderly and in renal dysfunction.

For urgent usage intravenous **ouabain** (if obtainable) may allow earlier benefit:

Dosage: 0.5–1.0 mg in 100 ml of 5 per cent dextrose over 1 hour.

Adverse effects: Intravenous digoxin is potentially toxic, and should be reserved for patients with a clear need for more rapid digitalization. Digoxin is a potent cause of nausea, and may be associated with vomiting and abdominal pain; it may also be responsible for just about any arrhythmia.

Digoxin overdose

Infusion of the digoxin-specific antibody fragment, F(ab), results in rapid reversal of the toxic effects of digoxin overdose. F(ab) fragments (Digibind) act by binding with digoxin, which is then excreted in the urine.

DISOPYRAMIDE

This antiarrhythmic agent has a similar electrophysiological profile to quinidine. It is useful in the management of both ventricular and supraventricular arrhythmias.

Dosage: *oral*: 300 mg loading dose; thereafter 100–200 mg 6-hourly. Slow-release formulations are available which allow 12-hourly dosing. The dose should be reduced in the elderly and in patients with renal failure.

Dosage: *IV* (slowly with ECG monitoring): 2 mg/kg over at least 5 minutes to a maximum of 150 mg.

Adverse effects: These are largely related to the anticholinergic effects of this agent, such as urinary retention and worsening of glaucoma. The agent is significantly negatively inotropic, and should be avoided in patients with overt or incipient cardiac failure.

DOBUTAMINE

A synthetic analogue of dopamine and a beta-adrenergic stimulating agent which does not stimulate dopaminergic receptors (such as in the kidney). It does appear to lack a chronotropic effect at low doses, where it appears to be a pure inotrope, and it appears to exert a greater lowering of pulmonary wedge pressure than dopamine.

Dosage: 1–10 micrograms/kg/minute (dosage above 10 micrograms/kg/minute results in undesirable vasoconstriction).

Its other advantage is that it can be administered via a peripheral line.

DOPAMINE

This is the precursor of noradrenaline, which is inotropic, and therefore is able to support the failing ventricle; in addition to which it activates dopaminergic receptors in the kidney, helping to preserve renal function in patients with low cardiac output. Dopamine must be given through a central line to avoid peripheral vasoconstriction and possible skin necrosis. It is chronotropic, especially at higher doses, and may therefore precipitate arrhythmias.

Dosage: 1–10 micrograms/kg/minute according to clinical response and effect on the heart rate. (Dosage above 10 micrograms/kg/minute results in undesirable vasoconstriction.)

A combination of dopamine and dobutamine may be useful in combining the favourable effects of both agents on cardiac output, pulmonary wedge pressure, and renal perfusion.

ENOXIMONE

This phosphodiesterase inhibitor acts by increasing cyclic AMP in the myocardium, resulting in a positive inotropic and vasodilatory effect.

Dosage: 90 micrograms/kg/minute intravenously over 10–30 minutes, followed by continuous or intermittent infusion of 5–20 micrograms/kg/minute. Total dosing over 24 hours should not exceed 24 mg/kg.

Adverse effects: It may be associated with arrhythmias, particularly in patients with pre-existing rhythm disturbance and with hypotension, in view of its vasodilatory effects.

FLECAINIDE

This agent is indicated in the management of chronic ventricular arrhythmias, but is also useful in the management of AV nodal re-entry arrhythmias. It is available both orally and parenterally.

Dosage: *IV*: 1–2 mg/kg over 10 minutes, then 0.15–0.25 mg/kg/hour. The maximum recommended bolus dose is 150 mg.

Dosage: *orally*: 100–200 mg twice daily.

Adverse effects: potentially this agent can give rise to heart block, because of its AV nodal effects. Some caution should be exercised in treating patients with cardiac failure, because of the negative inotropic effects of this drug; and nausea and dizziness may be experienced.

Flecainide should not be used for the management of arrhythmias early after infarction, as it may be proarrhythmic in patients with acute ischaemia (CAST investigators 1986).

ISOPRENALINE

The chronotropic effects of this agent are useful in profound, refractory bradycardia or in heart block whilst awaiting the insertion of a pacing electrode.

Dosage: 4 mg of isoprenaline in 500 ml of 5 per cent dextrose administered intravenously, according to effect on heart rate.

Adverse effects: tachycardia, arrhythmias, sweating, hypotension (vasodilation), headache, tremor.

LIGNOCAINE

This is the standard treatment for ventricular arrhythmias, including sustained ventricular tachycardia, and following ventricular fibrillation. It is used intravenously, because there is considerable first-pass metabolism in the liver.

Dosage: in order to raise blood levels rapidly, a bolus of 1−2 mg/kg is administered, followed by an infusion of 2−4 mg per minute for 12 hours, or as clinically indicated.

Adverse effects: Toxicity can occur within the therapeutic range, and drug clearance is reduced in the elderly, in cardiac failure, and in hepatic disease.

Toxicity can result in hypotension, bradycardia and nausea, vomiting, and convulsions.

MAGNESIUM

Magnesium should be administered to patients with hypokalaemia who have refractory or threatening arrhythmias. It appears to exert cardioprotective effects, and in particular may be inhibiting calcium influx into myocardial cells, may be reducing peripheral resistance, and, by increasing the threshold for electrical excitation of myocardial cells, reduces the likelihood of a current of injury's giving rise to an excitable focus near the infarct zone (Teo *et al.* 1992). The ISIS-4 study, which is currently (1992) recruiting, is investigating the role of routine magnesium in patients after infarction.

Dosage: 8 mmol of magnesium sulphate over 15 minutes (via an infusion pump or diluted in 100 ml of 5 per cent dextrose), followed by 72 mmol over 24 hours (via an infusion pump or diluted in 1 litre of 5 per cent dextrose).

MEXILETINE

This agent, which is available both orally and parenterally, has similar electrophysiological properties (and therefore indications) to lignocaine, and is used in the management of ventricular arrhythmias.

Dosage: *IV*: 100−250 mg at 12.5 mg/minute. Then 2.0 mg/kg/hour for 3.5 hours, and then 0.5 mg/kg/hour.

Dosage: *orally*: 100–400 mg 8-hourly.

Adverse effects: It may be associated with bradycardia, hypotension, and gastrointestinal upset. Neurological effects may be quite frequent, and tremor, dizziness, ataxia, confusion, and diplopia are sometimes associated with this drug.

MILRINONE

This phosphodiesterase inhibitor has inotropic and vasodilatory effects. It may be useful in the short-term management of patients with low output conditions.

Dosage: a loading dose should be used at 50 micrograms/kg over 10 minutes IV, followed by a maintenance infusion of 0.375–0.75 micrograms/kg/minute according to benefit. The total daily dose should not exceed 1.13 mg/kg.

Adverse effects: It may be associated with arrhythmias and in view of its vasodilatory effects it may result in lowering of blood pressure.

NALOXONE

This opioid antagonist may be used for the partial or complete reversal of opioid-induced respiratory depression.

Dosage: 0.8 mg IV. If the desired effect is not obtained, further 0.8 mg doses may be repeated after 5 minutes, up to a maximum of 10 mg. (The desired analgesic effect of the opiate may also be reversed by naloxone.)

NITRATES

These agents act mostly as venodilators, and result in reduction in left ventricular filling pressure and therefore cardiac work. They are widely used in the management of cardiac pain, but also to limit infarct size in acute myocardial infarction, and may be useful in the management of cardiac failure, in view of their favourable effects on cardiac haemodynamics.

Because of the rapid development of nitrate tolerance in **chronic** therapy, a 'nitrate break' must be provided, by prescribing nitrates for the twelve most symptomatic hours of the day, followed by a nitrate-free period.

Intravenous GTN has advantages over isosorbide, in that its shorter half life may increase safety when larger doses are employed.

Dosage: 0.6–10.0 mg/hour IV.

Whilst setting up an infusion, early clinical benefit may result from the use of GTN spray (1–4 puffs on to the tongue).

A fall of 20 mm Hg in systolic pressure or a sustained rise in heart rate is an indication to reduce the infusion rate.

Sustained release GTN in buccal form (the medication is placed between the upper lip and the gum) is a useful alternative to intravenous nitrates, avoiding the need for an intravenous infusion, especially in centres where infusion pumps are not readily available.

NITROPRUSSIDE

This vasodilator has balanced venous and arteriolar effects, and is a powerful vasodilator in the management of advanced left ventricular failure. It acts by favourably reducing venous return, and it increases cardiac output by decreasing arterial vascular resistance. As a result atrial and ventricular volumes decrease, as does left ventricular end-diastolic pressure, and this allows improved coronary endocardial perfusion and a reduction in myocardial oxygen consumption. It has a very rapid onset and cessation of effect, and therefore should only be used with invasive monitoring, as the effect on reduction of preload and blood-pressure can be rapid and excessive.

Dosage: an initial infusion of 10 micrograms/minute may be increased by 10 micrograms/minute every 10 minutes up to 200 micrograms/minute, according to haemodynamic benefit and the effect on pressure.

Adverse effects: Nitroprusside should not be withdrawn abruptly, because of the possibility of rebound hypertension. The solution must be freshly made up and protected from light, being discarded after 4 hours or sooner if discoloured: cyanide may accumulate with prolonged high doses (especially in patients with hepatic dysfunction), leading to lactic acidosis, and toxicity can be avoided by monitoring blood lactate and thiocyanate levels. Clinical manifestations of thiocyanate toxicity are: nausea, anorexia, hiccoughing, muscular spasm, confusion, and psychotic behaviour.

PROCAINAMIDE

This drug may suppress ventricular arrhythmias that remain refractory to lignocaine. It acts by reducing cardiac muscle excitability, increasing the ventricular threshold, and slowing conduction through ventricular muscle.

Procainamide should not be used in patients with atrioventricular block.

Dosage: *IV*: 50–100 mg slowly every 5–10 minutes under ECG and blood-pressure monitoring until the arrhythmia is suppressed or a maximum of one gram of procainamide has been given. Following the loading dose an infusion of 2–5 mg/minute should be started.

Dosage: *oral*: a break of about four hours is recommended before embarking on oral therapy at 250–500 mg every 4 hours (frequent dosing is required because of relatively rapid elimination).

Adverse effects: These include nausea, vomiting, confusion, rash, fever, agranulocytosis, and a lupus-like syndrome. Renal disease requires a reduction in dosage. Rapid intravenous administration may be associated with hypotension, sinus arrest, and heart block.

PROPAFENONE

This agent is indicated for the prophylaxis and treatment of ventricular arrhythmias. It slows conduction in the atria, AV node, and His–Purkinje system, and lengthens the PR interval and QRS duration on the surface electrocardiogram. It also prolongs the refractory period and slows conduction in accessory pathways in both directions, and may have a role in the management of re-entry tachycardia.

Dosage (70 kg and over): 150 mg three times daily after food, under hospital supervision using ECG and blood-pressure control. This may be increased at intervals of more than 3 days to 300 mg twice daily, and if required to a maximum of 300 mg three times daily. In the elderly or in those under 70 kg the dose should be reduced.

Adverse effects: propafenone is contraindicated in uncontrolled cardiac failure, severe bradycardia, and severe obstructive airways disease, and should be avoided in patients with conduction block unless they are adequately paced. Additional side-effects are constipation, blurred vision, dry mouth, nausea and vomiting, fatigue, bitter taste, diarrhoea, and headache. Propafenone increases the plasma levels of digoxin and warfarin, and the level of propafenone may be increased by concomitant use of cimetidine.

SALBUTAMOL

This beta-agonist causes arteriolar dilatation, and therefore increases cardiac output by reducing peripheral resistance.

Dosage: *IV*: 10–20 micrograms/minute, attempting to avoid tachycardia, which is undesirable in the presence of acute myocardial ischaemia.

Adverse effects: It may result in tremor and restlessness.

THROMBOLYTICS

This subject is covered in detail in Chapter 5, **hospital management**.

Dosage of thrombolytic agents:

- **Anistreplase:** *IV*: 30 units over 3–5 minutes.
- **Streptokinase:** *IV*: 1.5 megaunits over one hour.
- **tPA:** *IV*: 100 mg (10 per cent by intravenous bolus, 50 per cent by infusion over one hour, and the remaining 40 per cent over the subsequent 2 hours. In patients who are less than 67 kg the total dose should be 1.5 mg/kg). This agent requires the use of heparin, in view of its short half life.

References

Aarons, E. J. and Beeching, N. J. (1991). Survey of 'Do not resuscitate' orders in a district general hospital. *British Medical Journal*, **303**, 1504−6.

Aberg, A., Bergstrand, R., Johanssen, S., Ulvenstam, G., and Vedin, A. (1983). Cessation of smoking after myocardial infarction. Effects on mortality after 10 years. *British Heart Journal*, **49**, 416−22.

ASSET Study Group (1988). Trial of tissue plasminogen activator for mortality reduction in acute myocardial infarction: Anglo-Scandinavian study of early thrombolysis. *Lancet*, **ii**, 525−30.

Bradford, R. H., Shear, C. L., Chremos, A. N., Dujoune, C., Franklin, F., Hesney, M., *et al*. (1990). Expanded clinical evaluation of lovastatin (EXCEL) study: design and patient characteristics of a double-blind, placebo-controlled study in patients with moderate hypercholesterolemia. *American Journal of Cardiology*, **66**, 44B−55B.

British Cardiac Society Working Group on Coronary Prevention: conclusions and recommendations (1987). *British Heart Journal*, **57**(2), 188−9.

British Heart Foundation Working Group (1989). Role of the general practitioner in managing patients with myocardial infarction: impact of thrombolytic treatment. *British Medical Journal*, **299**, 555−6.

Brown, G., Albers, J. J., Fisher, L. D., Schaefer, S. M., Lin, J. T., Kaplan, C., *et al*. (1990). Regression of coronary artery disease as a result of intensive lipid-lowering therapy in men with high levels of apolipoprotein B. *New England Journal of Medicine*, **323**, 1289−98.

Brush, J. E., Brand, D. A., Acampora, D., Chalmer, B., and Wackers, F. J. (1985). Use of the initial electrocardiogram to predict in-hospital complications of acute myocardial infarction. *New England Journal of Medicine*, **312**, 1137−41.

Buchwald, H., Varco, R. L., Matts, J. P., Long, J. M., Fitch, L. L., Campbell, G. S., *et al*. (1990). Effect of partial ileal bypass surgery on mortality and morbidity from coronary heart disease in patients with hypercholesterolemia: report of the Programme on Surgical Control of the Hyperlipidemias (POSCH). *New England Journal of Medicine*, **323**, 946−55.

Burns, J. M. A., Hogg, K. J., Rae, A. P., Hillis, W. S., and Dunn, F. G. (1989). Impact of a policy of direct admission to a coronary care unit on use of thrombolytic treatment. *British Heart Journal*, **61**, 322−5.

Cairns, J. A., Gent, M., Singer, J., Finnie, K. J., Froggatt, G. M., Holder, D. A., *et al.* (1985). Aspirin, Sulfinpyrazone, or both in unstable angina: results of a Canadian multicentre trial. *New England Journal of Medicine*, **313**, 1369–75.

Califf, R. M. and Harrelson-Woodlief, S. L. (1990). At home thrombolysis. *Journal of the American College of Cardiology*, **15**, 937–9.

Campbell, R. W. F., Higham, D., Adams, P., and Murray, A. (1987). Potassium—its relevance for arrhythmias complicating acute myocardial infarction. *Journal of Cardiovascular Pharmacology*, **10**, S25–7.

Campbell, S., Hern, R. A., Quigley, P., Vincent, R., Jewitt, D., and Chamberlain, D. (1988). Identification of patients at low risk of dying after acute myocardial infarction, by simple clinical and submaximal exercise test criteria. *European Heart Journal*, **9**, 938–47.

CAST (Cardiac Arrhythmia Suppression Trial) Investigators (1986). Effect of encainide and flecainide on mortality in a randomised trial of arrhythmia suppression after myocardial infarction. *New England Journal of Medicine*, **216**, 406–12.

Castaigne, A. D., Herve, C., Douval-Moulin, A.-D., Gaillard, M., Dubois-Rande, J. L., Boesch, C., *et al.* (1989). Prehospital use of APSAC: results of a placebo-controlled study. *American Journal of Cardiology*, **64**, 30A–33A.

Chaitman, B. R., Fisher, L. D., Bourassa, M. G., Davis, K., Rogers, W. J., Maynard, C., *et al.* (1981). Effect of coronary bypass surgery on survival patterns in subsets of patients with left main coronary artery disease: report of the Collaborative Study in Coronary Artery Surgery (CASS). *American Journal of Cardiology*, **48**, 765–77.

Cobbe, S. M., Redmond, M. J., Watson, J. M., Hollingworth, J., and Carrington, D. (1991). 'Heartstart Scotland'—initial experience of a national scheme for out of hospital defibrillation. *British Medical Journal*, **303**, 1517–20.

Cohn, P. F. (1987). Total ischaemic burden: pathophysiology and prognosis. *American Journal of Cardiology*, **59**, 3C–6C.

Collins, R. and Julian, D. (1992). British Heart Foundation surveys (1987 and 1989) of United Kingdom treatment policies for acute myocardial infarction. *British Heart Journal*, **66**, 250–5.

Colquhoun, M. C. (1988). Use of defibrillators by general practitioners. *British Medical Journal*, **297**, 336.

Colquhoun, M. C. (1989). General practitioner's use of electrocardiography: relevance to early thrombolytic treatment. *British Medical Journal*, **299**, 433.

Committee on Medical Aspects of Food Policy (1984). *Diet and cardiovascular disease*. HMSO, London.

Cross, S. J., Lee, H. S., Rawles, J. M., and Jennings, K. (1991). Safety of thrombolysis in association with cardiopulmonary resuscitation. *British Medical Journal*, **303**, 1242.

Cross, S., Lee, H. S., Kenmure, A., Walton, S., and Jennings, K. (1992). Should every patient under 60 with acute myocardial infarction undergo cardiac catheterisation? Experience with a consecutive series of patients. *Journal of the American College of Cardiology*, **19**, No.3, 81A.

Cummins, R. O., Eisenberg, M. S., Hallstrom, A. P., and Litwin, P. E. (1985). Survival of out-of-hospital cardiac arrest with early initiation of cardiopulmonary resuscitation. *American Journal of Emergency Medicine*, **3**, 114–19.

Daggett, W. M. (1978). Surgical management of ventricular septal defects complicating myocardial infarction. *World Journal of Surgery*, **2**, 753– 64.

DAVIT-I. Danish Study Group on Verapamil in Myocardial Infarction (1984). Verapamil in acute myocardial infarction. *European Heart Journal*, **5**, 516–28.

DAVIT-II. Danish Study Group on Verapamil in Myocardial Infarction (1990). Effect of verapamil on mortality and major events after acute myocardial infarction. *American Journal of Cardiology*, **66**, 779–85.

Davies, A. (1989). Electrocardiographs in general practice. *British Medical Journal*, **299**, 408.

Davies, S. W., Marchant, B., Lyons, J. P., Timmis, A. D., Rothman, M. T., Layton, C. A., *et al.* (1990). Coronary lesion morphology in acute myocardial infarction: demonstration of early remodelling after streptokinase treatment. *Journal of the American College of Cardiology*, **16**, 1079–86.

Deanfield, J. E., Maseri, A., Selwyn, A. P., Ribeiro, P., Chierchia, S., Krikler, S., *et al.* (1983). Myocardial ischaemia during daily life in patients with stable angina: its relation to symptoms and heart rate changes. *Lancet*, **i**, 753–8.

De Servi, S., Berzuini, C., Poma, E., Ferrario, M., Ghio, S., Scire, A., *et al.* (1989). Long-term survival and risk stratification in patients with angina at rest undergoing medical treatment. *International Journal of Cardiology*, **22**, 43–50.

DeWood, M. A., Spores, J., Notske, R., Mouser, L. T., Burroughs, R., Golden, M. S., *et al.* (1980). Prevalence of total coronary occlusion during the early hours of transmural myocardial infarction. *New England Journal of Medicine*, **303**, 897–902.

de Zwaan, C., Bar, F. W., Janssen, J. H., Cheriex, E. C., Dassen, W. R., Brugada, P., *et al.* (1989). Angiographic and clinical characteristics of patients with unstable angina showing an ECG pattern indicating critical narrowing of the proximal LAD coronary artery. *American Heart Journal*, **117**, 657–65.

Dickey, W., Dalzell, G. W. N., McC. Anderson, J., and Adgey, A. A. J. (1992). The accuracy of decision-making of a semi-automatic defibrillator during cardiac arrest. *European Heart Journal*, **13**, 608–15.

Dracup, K., Guzy, P. M., Taylor, S. E., and Barry, J. (1986). Cardiopulmonary resuscitation (CPR) training: consequences for family members of high-risk cardiac patients. *Archives of Internal Medicine*, **146**, 1757–61.

Dunkman, W. B., Leinbach, R. C., Buckley, M. J., Mundth, E. D., Kantrowitz, A. R., Austen, W. G., *et al.* (1972). Clinical and hemodynamic results of intra-aortic balloon pumping and surgery for cardiogenic shock. *Circulation*, **46**, 465–77.

Dwyer, J. and Hetzel, B. S. (1980). A comparison of trends of coronary heart disease mortality in Australia, USA and England and Wales with reference to three major risk factors—hypertension, cigarette smoking and diet. *International Journal of Epidemiology*, **9**, 65–71.

Edmunds, L. H. (1982). Thromboembolic complications of current cardiac valvular prostheses. *Annals of Thoracic Surgery*, **34**, 96–106.

EMERAS Trial Study Group (1991). Presented American College of Cardiology, Atlanta, March 1991.

EMIP Subcommittee (1988). Potential time saving with pre-hospital intervention in acute myocardial infarction. *European Heart Journal*, **9**, 118–24.

EMIP Investigators (1992). The European Myocardial Infarction Project, American College of Cardiology, Dallas, April 1992.

European Coronary Surgery Study Group (1980). Prospective randomised study of coronary artery bypass surgery in stable angina pectoris: second interim report. *Lancet*, **ii**, 491–5.

Fineberg, H. V., Scadden, D., and Goldman, L. (1984). Care of patients with a low probability of acute myocardial infarction. *New England Journal of Medicine*, **310**, 1301–7.

Fioretti, P., Baardman, T., Deckers, J., Salm, E., Zivers, G., Kazemier, M., *et al.* (1988). Social fate and long survival of patients with a recent myocardial infarction after cardiac rehabilitation. *European Heart Journal*, **9**(suppl L), 89–94.

Fitzpatrick, B., Watt, G. C. M., and Tunstall-Pedoe, H. (1992). Potential impact of emergency intervention on sudden deaths from coronary heart disease in Glasgow. *British Heart Journal*, **67**, 250–4.

Fowler, N. O. (1971). Autoimmune heart disease. *Circulation*, **44**, 159–62.

Friedman, M., Thoresen, C. E., Gill, J. J., Ulmer, D., Thompson, L., Powell, L., *et al.* (1982). Feasibility of altering Type A behaviour pattern after myocardial infarction. *Circulation*, **66**, 83–92.

Fromer, M., Brachmann, J., Block, M., Siebels, J., Hoffmann, E., and Almendral, J. (1992). Efficacy of automatic multimodal device therapy for ventricular tachyarrhythmias as delivered by a new implantable pacing cardioverter–defibrillator. *Circulation*, **86**, 363–74.

Fulton, M., Lutz, W., Donald, K. W., Kirby, B. J., Duncan, B., Morrison, S. L., *et al.* (1972). Natural history of unstable angina. *Lancet*, **i**, 860–5.

Fuster, V. and Halperin, J. L. (1989). Left ventricular thrombi and cerebral embolism: an emerging approach. *New England Journal of Medicine*, **320**, 392–4.

Gazes, P. C., Mobley, E. M., Faris, H. M., Duncan, R. C., and Humphries, G. B. (1973). Preinfarctional (unstable) angina—a prospective study—ten year follow-up. Prognostic significance of electrocardiographic changes. *Circulation*, **48**, 331–7.

Gerstenblith, G., Ouyang, P., Achuff, S. C., Bulkley, B. H., Becker, L. C., Mellits, E. D., *et al.* (1982). Nifedipine in unstable angina: a double-blind, randomised trial. *New England Journal of Medicine*, **306**, 885–9.

Gibson, R. S., Boden, W. E., Theroux, P., Strauss, H. D., Pratt, C. M., Gheorghiade, M., *et al.* (1986). Diltiazem and reinfarction in patients with non-Q-wave myocardial infarction. *New England Journal of Medicine*, **315**, 423–9.

GISSI Trial Study Group (1986). Effectiveness of intravenous thrombolytic treatment in acute myocardial infarction. *Lancet*, **i**, 397–402.

Goldberg, R. J., Gore, J. M., Alpert, J. S., Osganian, V., De Groot, J., Bade, J., *et al.* (1991). Cardiogenic shock after acute myocardial infarction—incidence and mortality from a community-wide perspective 1975–1988. *New England Journal of Medicine*, **325**, 1117–22.

Goldman, L., Weinberg, M., Weisberg, M., Olshen, R., Cook, E. F., Sargent, R. K., *et al.* (1982). A computer-derived protocol to aid in the diagnosis of emergency room patients with acute chest pain. *New England Journal of Medicine*, **307**, 588–96.

Goldman, L., Cook, E. F., and Brand, D. A. (1988). A computer protocol to predict myocardial infarction in emergency department patients with chest pain. *New England Journal of Medicine*, **318**, 797–803.

Gottlieb, S. O., Weisfeldt, M. L., Ouyang, P., Mellits, E. D., and Gerstenblith, G. (1986). Silent ischaemia as a marker for early unfavourable outcomes in patients with unstable angina. *New England Journal of Medicine*, **314**, 1214–19.

Gray, W. A., Capone, R. J., and Most, A. S. (1991). Unsuccessful medical resuscitation—are continued efforts in the emergency department justified? *New England Journal of Medicine*, **325**, 1393–8.

GREAT Study Group (1992). Feasibility, safety, and efficacy of domiciliary thrombolysis by general practitioners: Grampian region early anistreplase trial. *British Medical Journal*, **305**, 548–53.

Greenland, P. and Chu, J. S. (1988). Efficacy of cardiac rehabilitation services with emphasis on patients after myocardial infarction. *Annals of Internal Medicine*, **109**, 650–63.

Gwilt, D. J., Nattrass, M., and Pentecost, B. L. (1982). Use of low-dose insulin infusion in diabetics after myocardial infarction. *British Medical Journal*, **285**, 1402–4.

Held, A. C., Cole, P. L., Lipton, B., Gore, J. M., Antman, E. M., Hochman, J. S., *et al.* (1988). Rupture of the interventricular septum complicating acute myocardial infarction: a multicentre analysis of clinical findings and outcome. *American Heart Journal*, **116**, 1330–6.

Hjermann, I., Velve Byre, K., Holme, I., and Leren, P. (1981). Effect of diet and smoking intervention on the incidence of coronary heart disease: report from the Oslo study group of a randomised trial in healthy men. *Lancet*, **ii**, 1303–10.

Hutchins, G. M. (1979). Rupture of the interventricular septum complicating myocardial infarction: pathological analysis of 10 patients with clinically diagnosed perforations. *American Heart Journal*, **97**, 165–73.

ISIS-1 Collaborative Group (1988). Mechanisms for the early mortality reduction produced by beta-blockade started early in acute myocardial infarction: ISIS-1. *Lancet*, **i**, 921–3.

ISIS-2 Collaborative Group (1988). Randomised trial of intravenous streptokinase, oral aspirin, both or neither amongst 17 187 cases of suspected acute myocardial infarction: ISIS-2. *Lancet*, **ii**, 349–60.

ISIS-3 Collaborative Group (1992). ISIS-3: a randomised comparison of streptokinase vs tissue plasminogen activator vs anistreplase and of aspirin alone among 41 299 cases of suspected acute myocardial infarction. *Lancet*, **339**, 753–70.

Jennings, K., Reid, D. S., and Julian, D. G. (1983). 'Reciprocal' ST depression, exercise induced ST depression and coronary pathology. *British Medical Journal*, **287**, 634–7.

Jennings, K., Reid, D. S., Hawkins, T., and Julian, D. G. (1984). Role of exercise testing early after myocardial infarction in identifying candidates for coronary surgery. *British Medical Journal*, **288**, 185–7.

Jugdutt, B. I. and Sivaram, C. A. (1989). Prospective two-dimensional echocardiographic evaluation of left ventricular thrombus and embolism after acute myocardial infarction. *Journal of the American College of Cardiology*, **13**(3), 554–64.

Kannel, W. B. and Abbott, R. D. (1984). Incidence and prognosis of unrecognised myocardial infarction. *New England Journal of Medicine*, **311**, 1144–7.

Kannel, W. B., Thom, T. J., and Hurst, J. W. (1986). Incidence, prevalence and mortality of cardiovascular diseases. In *The heart* (6th edn, ed. J. W. Hurst), p. 560. McGraw-Hill, New York.

Keys, A. (1980). *Seven countries*. Harvard University Press, Cambridge, Mass.

Kokott, N., Rutsch, W., Berghofer, G., Loos, D., Dreysse, S., Dougherty, C., *et al.* (1990). Pre-hospital treatment with IV rt-PA in acute myocardial infarction. *European Heart Journal*, **11**(suppl), 356.

Laffel, G. L., Fineberg, H. V., and Braunwald, E. (1987). A cost-effectiveness model for coronary thrombolysis/reperfusion therapy. *Journal of the American College of Cardiology*, **10**, 79B–90B.

Lee, T. H., Royan, G. W., Weisberg, M. C., Brand, D. A., Acampora, D., Stasiulewicz, A. A., *et al.* (1987). Clinical characteristics and natural history of patients with acute myocardial infarction sent home from the emergency room. *American Journal of Cardiology*, **60**, 219–24.

Lee, L., Bates, E. R., Pitt, B., Walton, J. A., Laufer, N., and O'Neill, W. W. (1988). Percutaneous transluminal coronary angioplasty improves survival in acute myocardial infarction complicated by cardiogenic shock. *Circulation*, **78**, 1345–51.

Lee, H. S., Cross, S. J., Davidson, R., Reid, T., and Jennings, K. P. (1992*a*). When is it safe to readminister streptokinase for acute myocardial infarction? Measurement of early and late antistreptokinase antibody and neutralisation titres. *Journal of the American College of Cardiology*, **19**, No.3, 179A.

Lee, H. S., Cross, S. J., Rawles, J. M., and Jennings, K. P. (1992*b*). Patients with suspected myocardial infarction who present with ST depression—patient characteristics, ECG findings and prognosis. *European Heart Journal*, **13**, 446.

Lee, H. S., Cross, S. J., Garthwaite, P., and Jennings, K. P. (1992*c*). Rapid exclusion of acute myocardial infarction in patients without ST elevation using serial enzyme analysis with novel analysers—myoglobin, creatine kinase and creatine kinase-MB enzymes. British Cardiac Society, Harrogate, May 1992.

Lee, H. S., Yule, S., McKenzie, A., Cross, S. J., Davidson, R. J. L., Reid, T., *et al.* (1992*d*). Hypersensitivity reactions to streptokinase in patients with high pre-treatment antistreptokinase antibody and neutralisation titres—experience with 189 consecutive patients with suspected myocardial infarction. British Cardiac Society, Harrogate, May 1992.

Lewis, H. D., Davis, J. M., Archibald, D. G., Steinke, W. E., Smitherman, T. C., Doherty, J. E., *et al.* (1983). Protective effects of aspirin against acute myocardial infarction and death in men with unstable angina. *New England Journal of Medicine*, **309**, 396–403.

Lipkin, D. P. (1991). Is cardiac rehabilitation necessary? *British Heart Journal*, **65**, 237–8.

Luchi, R. J., Scott, S. M., and Deupree, R. H. (1987). Comparison of medical and surgical treatment for unstable angina pectoris. *New England Journal of Medicine*, **316**, 977–84.

Madigan, N. P., Rutherford, B. D., and Frye, R. L. (1976). The clinical course, early prognosis and coronary anatomy of subendocardial infarction. *American Journal of Medicine*, **60**, 634–41.

Mair, J., Artner-Dworzak, E., Lechleitner, P., Smidt, J., Wagner, I., Dienstl, F., *et al.* (1991). Cardiac troponin T in diagnosis of acute myocardial infarction. *Clinical Chemistry*, **37**, 845–52.

Marmot, M. G. (1984). Alcohol and coronary heart disease. *International Journal of Epidemiology*, **13**, 160–7.

Mathewson, Z. M., McCloskey, B. G., Evans, A. E., Russell, C. J., and Wilson, C. (1985). Mobile coronary care and community mortality from myocardial infarction. *Lancet*, **i**, 441–4.

McNeill, A. J., Cunningham, S. R., Flannery, D. J., Dalzell, G. W., Wilson, C. M., Campbell, N. P., *et al.* (1989). A double-blind placebo controlled study of early and late administration of recombinant tissue plasminogen activator in acute myocardial infarction. *British Heart Journal*, **61**, 316–21.

Meade, T. W., Chakrabarti, R., Haines, A. P., North, W. R. S., and Stirling, Y. (1980). Haemostatic function and cardiovascular death: early results of a prospective study. *Lancet*, **i**, 1050–4.

Medical Commission On Accident Prevention (1985). *Medical aspects of fitness to drive*. HMSO, London.

Metcalfe, M. J., Paterson, N., Smith, F. W., and Jennings, K. (1988). Does cardioversion for atrial fibrillation result in myocardial damage? *British Medical Journal*, **296**, 1364.

Monpère, C., François, G., and Broudier, M. (1988). Effects of comprehensive rehabilitation programme in patients with three vessel coronary disease. *European Heart Journal*, **9**(suppl M), 28–31.

Morley, J. E. and Reese, S. S. (1989). Clinical implications of the aging heart. *American Journal of Medicine*, **86**, 77–86.

Morris, J. N., Pollard, R., Everitt, M. G., and Chave, S. P. W. (1980). Vigorous exercise in leisure time: protection against coronary heart disease. *Lancet*, **ii**, 1207–10.

Mulcahy, R., Al Awahdi, A. H. L., de Buitleor, M., Tobin, G., Johnson, H., and Contoy, R. (1985). Natural history and prognosis of unstable angina. *American Heart Journal*, **109**, 753–8.

Muller, J., Morrison, J., Stone, P., Rude, R. E., Rosner, B., Roberts, R., *et al.* (1984). Nifedipine therapy for patients with threatened and acute myocardial infarction: a randomised, double-blind, placebo-controlled comparison. *Circulation*, **69**, 740–7.

Muller, J. E., Stone, P. H., Turi, Z. G., Rutherford, J. D., Czeisler, C. A., Parker, C., *et al.* (1985). Circadian variation in the frequency of onset of myocardial infarction. *New England Journal of Medicine*, **313**, 1315–22.

Muller, J. E., Rude, R. E., Braunwald, E., Hartwell, T. D., Roberts, R., Sobel, B. E., *et al.* (1988). Myocardial infarct extension: Occurrence, outcome and risk factors in the multicentre investigation of limitation of infarct size. *Annals of Internal Medicine*, **108**, 1–6.

Mulley, A. G., Thibault, G. E., Hughes, R. A., Barnett, G. O., Reder, V. A., and Sherman, E. L. (1980). The course of patients with suspected myocardial infarction. *New England Journal of Medicine*, **302**, 943–8.

Multicentre Diltiazem Postinfarction Trial Group (1988). The effect of dilti-azem on mortality and reinfarction after myocardial infarction. *New England Journal of Medicine*, **319**, 385–92.

O'Connor, G. T., Buring, J. E., Yusuf, Y., Goldhaber, S. Z., Olmstead, E. M., Paffenburger, R. S., *et al.* (1989). An overview of randomised trials of rehabilitation with exercise after myocardial infarction. *Circulation*, **80**, 234–44.

Ohman, E. M., Califf, R. M., Topol, E. J., Candela, R., Abbottsmith, C., Ellis, S., *et al.* (1990). Consequences of reocclusion after successful reper-fusion therapy in acute myocardial infarction. *Circulation*, **82**, 781–91.

Oliver, M. F. (1992). Doubts about preventing coronary heart disease. *British Medical Journal*, **304**, 393–4.

Olsen, O. and Kristensen, T. S. (1991). Impact of work environment on cardiovascular diseases in Denmark. *Journal of Epidemiology and Com-munity Health*, **45**, 4–10.

Page, D. L., Caulfield, J. B., Kastor, J. A., DeSanctis, R. W., and Sanders, C. A. (1971). Myocardial changes associated with cardiogenic shock. *New England Journal of Medicine*, **285**, 133–7.

Pai, G. R., Haites, N. E., and Rawles, J. M. (1987). One thousand heart attacks in Grampian: the place of cardiopulmonary resuscitation in general practice. *British Medical Journal*, **294**, 352–4.

Pell, A. C. H., Miller, H. C., Robertson, C. E., and Fox, K. A. A. (1992). Effect of 'fast track' admission for acute myocardial infarction on delay to thrombolysis. *British Medical Journal*, **304**, 83–7.

Pfeffer, M. A., Braunwald, E., Moye, L. A., Basta, L., Brown, E. J., Cuddy, T. E., *et al.* (1992). Effect of captopril on mortality and morbidity in patients with left ventricular dysfunction after myocardial infarction. *New England Journal of Medicine*, **327**, 669–77.

Phipps, C. (1936). Contributory causes of coronary thrombosis. *Journal of the American Medical Association*, **106**, 761–2.

Pohjola-Sinonen, S., Muller, J. E., Stone, P. H., Willich, S. N., Antman, E. N., Davis, V. G., *et al.* (1989). Ventricular septal and free wall rupture complicating acute myocardial infarction: experience in the multicentre investigation of limitation of infarct size. *American Heart Journal*, **117**, 809–18.

Pozen, M. W., D'Agostino, R. B., Mitchell, J. B., Rosenfeld, D. M., Guglielmino, J. T., Schwartz, M. L., *et al.* (1980). The usefulness of a predictive instrument to reduce inappropriate admissions to the coronary care unit. *Annals of Internal Medicine*, **92**, 238–42.

Pozen, M. W., D'Agostino, R. B., Selker, H. P., Sythowski, P. A., and Hood, W. B. (1984). A predictive instrument to improve coronary-care unit admission practices in acute ischaemic heart disease. *New England Journal of Medicine*, **310**, 1273–8.

Puleo, P. R., Guadagno, A. G., Roberts, R., Scheel, M. V., Marian, A. J., Churchill, D., *et al.* (1990). Early diagnosis of acute myocardial infarction based on assay for subforms of creatine kinase-MB. *Circulation*, **82**, 759–64.

Rankin, A. C., Oldroyd, K. G., Chong, E., Rae, A. P., and Cobbe, S. M. (1989). Value and limitations of adenosine in the diagnosis and treatment of narrow and broad complex tachycardias. *British Heart Journal*, **62**, 195–203.

Ratshin, R. A., Rackley, C. E., and Russell, R. O. (1972). Haemodynamic evaluation of left ventricular function in shock complicating myocardial infarction. *Circulation*, **45**, 127–39.

Rawles, J. M. (1987). General practitioner's management of acute myocardial infarction and cardiac arrest: relevance to thrombolytic therapy. *British Medical Journal*, **295**, 639–40.

Rawles, J. M. and Haites, N. E. (1988). Patient and general practitioner delays in acute myocardial infarction. *British Medical Journal*, **296**, 882–4.

Reilly, I. A. G. and Fitzgerald, G. A. (1987). Inhibition of thromboxane formation *in vivo* and *ex vivo*: implications for therapy with platelet inhibitory drugs. *Blood*, **69**, 180–6.

Ridker, P. M., Manson, J. A. E., Buring, J. E., Muller, J. E., and Hennekens, C. H. (1990). Circadian variation of acute myocardial infarction and the effect of low dose aspirin in a randomised trial of physicians. *Circulation*, **82**, 897–902.

Roberts, K. B., Califf, R. M., Harrell, F. E., Lee, K. L., Pryor, D. B., Rosati, R. A., *et al.* (1983). The prognosis for patients with new-onset angina who have undergone cardiac catheterisation. *Circulation*, **68**, 970–8.

Roth, A., Barbash, G. I., Hod, H., Miller, H. I., Rath, S., Modan, M., *et al.* (1990). Should thrombolytic therapy be administered in the mobile intensive care unit in patients with evolving myocardial infarction? A pilot study. *Journal of the American College of Cardiology*, **15**, 932–6.

Rowley, J. M., Mounser, P., Harrison, E. A., Skene, A. M., and Hampton, J. R. (1992). Management of myocardial infarction: implications for current policy derived from the Nottingham Heart Attack Register. *British Heart Journal*, **67**, 255–62.

RCGP (Royal College of General Practitioners) (1986). *Morbidity statistics from general practice 1981–1982, third national survey.* HMSO, London.

Royal College of Physicians (1987). Resuscitation from cardiopulmonary arrest. Training and Organization. A report of the Royal College of Physicians. *Journal of the Royal College of Physicians of London*, **21**, No.3, 175–82.

Ruberman, W., Weinblatt, E., Goldberg, J. D., and Chaudhary, B. S. (1984). Psychosocial influences on mortality after myocardial infarction. *New England Journal of Medicine*, **311**, 552–9.

Rude, R. E., Poole, K., Muller, J. E., Turi, Z., Rutherford, J., Parker, C., et al. (1983). Electrocardiographic and clinical criteria for recognition of acute myocardial infarction based on analysis of 3697 patients. *American Journal of Cardiology*, **52**, 936–42.

SCATI Study Group (1989). Randomised controlled trial of subcutaneous calcium heparin in acute myocardial infarction. *Lancet*, **ii**, 182–6.

Scott, S. M., Luchi, R. J., and Deupree, R. H. (1988). Veterans administration co-operative study for treatment of patients with unstable angina: results in patients with abnormal left ventricular function. *Circulation*, **78**, (suppl 1), 113–21.

Shanfield, S. B. (1990). Return to work after an acute myocardial infarction: a review. *Journal of Critical Care*, **19**, 109–17.

Shaper, A. G., Cook, D. G., Walker, M., and Macfarlane, P. W. (1984). Prevalence of ischaemic heart disease in middle aged British men. *British Heart Journal*, **51**, 595–605.

Shaper, A. G., Pocock, S. J., Walker, M., Philips, A. N., Whitehead, T. P., and MacFarlane, F. W. (1985). Risk factors for ischaemic heart disease: the prospective phase of the British Regional Heart Study. *Journal of Epidemiology and Community Health*, **39**, 197–209.

Sixty Plus Reinfarction Research Study Group (1980). A double-blind trial to assess long-term oral anticoagulant therapy in elderly patients after myocardial infarction. *Lancet*, **ii**, 980–94.

Smith, G. D. and Pekkanen, J. (1992). Should there be a moratorium on the use of cholesterol lowering drugs? *British Medical Journal*, **304**, 431–3.

SPRINT (Secondary Prevention Reinfarction Nifedipine Trial) Group (1988). A randomized intervention trial of nifedipine in patients with acute myocardial infarction. *European Heart Journal*, **9**, 354–64.

Strandberg, T. E., Salomaa, V. V., Naukkarinen, V. A., Vanhanen, H. T., Sarna, S. J., and Miettinen, T. A. (1991). Long-term mortality after 5-year multifactorial primary prevention of cardiovascular diseases in middle-aged men. *Journal of the American Medical Association*, **266**, 1225–9.

Swahn, E., Von Schank, H., and Wallentin, L. (1989). Plasma fibrinogen in unstable coronary artery disease. *Scandinavian Journal of Laboratory Investigation*, **49**, 49–54.

Swales, J. D., Ramsay, L. E., Coope, J. R., Pocock, S. J., Robertson, J. I. S., Sever, P. S., et al. (1989). Treating mild hypertension. Report of the British Hypertension Society working party. *British Medical Journal*, **298**, 694–8.

Taffet, G. E., Teasdale, T. A., and Luchi, R. J. (1988). In-hospital cardiopulmonary resuscitation. *Journal of the American Medical Association*, **260**, 2069–72.

Takaro, T., Hultgren, H. N., Lipton, M. J., and Detre, K. M. (1976). The VA randomised cooperative study of surgery for coronary arterial occlusive disease. 11. Subgroup with significant left main lesions. *Circulation*, **54**, (suppl 3), 107–17.

Telford, A. M. and Wilson, C. (1981). Trial of heparin versus atenolol in prevention of myocardial infarction in intermediate coronary syndrome. *Lancet*, **i**, 1225–8.

Teo, K. K., Yusuf, S., Collins, R., Held, P. H., and Peto, R. (1992). Effects of intravenous magnesium in suspected acute myocardial infarction: overview of randomised trials. *British Medical Journal*, **303**, 1499–1503.

Thompson, R. G., Hallstrom, A. P., and Cobb, L. A. (1979). Bystander-initiated cardiopulmonary resuscitation in the management of ventricular fibrillation. *Annals of Internal Medicine*, **90**, 737–40.

Thombolysis Early In Acute Heart Attack Trial Study Group (1990). Very early thrombolytic therapy in suspected acute myocardial infarction. *American Journal of Cardiology*, **65**, 401–7.

Tierney, W. M., Roth, B. J., and Psaty, B. (1985). Predictors of myocardial infarction in the emergency room patients. *Critical Care Medicine*, **13**, 526–31.

TIMI Study Group (1989). Comparison of invasive and conservative strategies after treatment with intravenous tissue plasminogen activator in acute myocardial infarction: results of the thrombolysis in myocardial infarction (TIMI) phase 11 trial. *New England Journal of Medicine*, **320**, 618–27.

Tofler, G. H., Muler, J. E., Stone, P. H., Wilich, S. N., Davis, V. G., and Poole, K. (1988). Factors leading to shorter survival after acute myocardial infarction in patients aged 65 to 75 years compared with younger patients. *American Journal of Cardiology*, **62**, 860–7.

Topol, E. J., Burek, K., O'Neill, W. W., Kewman, D. G., Kander, N. H., Shea, M. J., *et al.* (1988). A randomised controlled trial of hospital discharge three days after myocardial infarction in the era of reperfusion. *New England Journal of Medicine*, **318**, 1083–8.

Tunstall-Pedoe, H., Bailey, L., Chamberlain, D. A., Marsden, A. K., Ward, M. E., and Zideman, D. A. (1992). Survey of 3765 cardiopulmonary resuscitations in British hospitals (the BRESUS study): methods and overall results. *British Medical Journal*, **304**, 1347–51.

Turkulin, C., Cerevec, D., and Batorski, F. (1988). Predictive markers of occupational activity in 415 post myocardial infarction patients after one-year follow up. *European Heart Journal*, **9**(suppl L), 103–8.

Turpie, A. G. G., Robinson, J. G., Doyle, D. J., Muiji, A. S., Mishkel, G. J., Sealey, B. J., *et al.* (1989). Comparison of high-dose with low-dose subcutaneous heparin in the prevention of left ventricular mural thrombosis in patients with acute transmural anterior myocardial infarction. *New England Journal of Medicine*, **320**, 352–7.

Varma, S. K. and Gibson, R. S. (1987). Predischarge exercise ECG vs thallium-201 in predicting prognosis after non-Q wave myocardial infarction. *Circulation*, **76**(suppl 4), 157.

Vermeer, F., Simons, M. L., Van de Zwaan, C. E. G. A., Verheugt, F. W. A., Van der Laarse, A., *et al.* (1988). Cost benefit analysis of early thrombolytic treatment with intracoronary streptokinase. *British Heart Journal*, **59**, 527–34.

Vlodaver, Z. and Edwards, J. E. (1977). Rupture of the ventricular septum or papillary muscle complicating myocardial infarction. *Circulation*, **55**, 815–22.

Wallentin, L. *et al.* for The Risk Study Group In South East Sweden (1989). ASA 75 mg after an episode of unstable coronary artery disease—risk for myocardial infarct death in a randomized placebo-controlled study. *Circulation*, **80**(suppl 11), 419.

Weaver, W. D., Fahrenbruch, C. E., Johnson, D. D., Hallstrom, A. P., Cobb, L. A., and Copass, M. K. (1990). Effect of epinephrine and lidocaine therapy on outcome after cardiac arrest due to ventricular fibrillation. *Circulation*, **82**, 2027–34.

Weiner, D. A., Ryan, T. J., McCabe, C. H., Luk, S., Chaitman, B. R., Sheffield, L. T., *et al.* (1987). Significance of silent myocardial ischaemia during exercise testing in patients with coronary disease. *American Journal of Cardiology*, **59**, 725–9.

Wilcox, R. G. (1990). Thrombolysis and the general practitioner. Useful after careful evaluation of the patient. *British Medical Journal*, **300**, 869–70.

Willems, J. L., Willems, R. J., Willems, G. M., Arnold, A. E. R., Van De Werf, F., and Verstraete, M. (1990). For the European Cooperative Study Group for Recombinant tissue-type plasminogen activator. *Circulation*, **82**, 1147–58.

Yusuf, S., Collins, R., MacMahon, S., and Peto, R. (1988). Effects of intravenous nitrates on mortality in acute myocardial infarction: an overview of the randomised trials. *Lancet*, **i**, 1088–92.

Index